JUSTIFIABLE PRIDE

A
World War II
Memoir

William D. Stevens

ISBN 0-9673295-4-X

Printed in the United States of America
by
Service Press
Henderson, NE 68371

Cover photo of Diez Castle by Ann Lundy

JEMEL BOOKS

2340 DEVOE DRIVE
LINCOLN, NE 68506

Dedicated to

those whose lives

were disrupted

by

World War II

Contents

JUSTIFIABLE PRIDE

Foreword

This book describes my experiences as a soldier during the second World War, and the thoughts those experiences gave rise to – at the time and later. It's based on letters I wrote my parents and brothers, on what I recorded while a prisoner of war, and on memory. The last, after half a century, is not a dependable source, so I've relied on it only when neither of the other two exists or they are incomplete.

Ninety percent of the narrative that follows is an accurate, unembellished account of what actually occurred. The rest is essentially true but not entirely, because many of the excerpts from my letters and P.O.W. diaries have been edited to make them more understandable; occasionally, in describing something, details that may be more imaginary than real are included; in my account of attacks against enemy troops I combine events that took place at different times and involved other people; and for everybody below the rank of colonel, including myself, I have used a fictitious name. Mine isn't William D. Stevens and I wasn't a part of E Company.

You can find out, with very little effort, who I am and which of the 26th Infantry Division's rifle companies I did serve in, but why bother? Names are unimportant; it's what happened that counts.

Bill Stevens

Lincoln, Nebraska
September, 1998

Prologue

Ten days after my military service ended in January, 1946, a letter from the Commanding General of Army Ground Forces arrived. It said that in years to come I would "look back with justifiable pride" at what I did for my country.

Who decides whether what you did really mattered? The officers you served under? The soldiers you were in charge of? Those who fought beside you? Or does each individual decide for himself?

How is one's contribution measured? By how many of the enemy he killed? By his unit's successes? By the number of people he helped? By the sacrifices he made?

Is being proud of your participation in war – an enterprise that causes death, destruction and indescribable suffering – ever "justifiable"?

I

Nighttime in my dark, unlighted cell seemed interminable. The days were beginning to seem that way too. Cold, hungry and discouraged, I walked back and forth to keep my weakened body functioning and avoid despair. How long are they going to hold me here, I wondered. Until Allied forces crush Hitler's defending armies and enter their homeland? Maybe. Will that happen soon? Probably not; when I was captured, more than four weeks ago, we were a long way from the border.

Is my interrogator bluffing when he says I'll be sent to "a worse place" if his questions aren't answered? How long can I put up with this psychologically? How long until I break down physically? What am I supposed to do? How did a tolerant, fun-loving boy from Nebraska end up in solitary confinement in an ancient castle in Germany? The loneliness of my room, with its clammy stone walls and eerie silence, was getting to me.

I tried to buoy myself by recalling events from bygone days: catching my first fish when I was seven, licking the bowl after Mom made icing for a cake, how thrilled I was in high school when the girl I secretly liked kissed me after a Job's Daughters dance, how lonely and betrayed I felt when it became apparent that she cared for somebody else, how quickly joy returned as new vistas opened and my shyness began to disappear.

Memories came of my first week at our state university in

September of 1938. During Military Science class, the rifle I was using to learn "Right Shoulder, Arms" slipped from my hands and landed butt-first on a toe, causing excruciating pain. I wanted to cry out in agony; but aware that a tough old sergeant was silently watching, grit my teeth, retrieved it, and continued as if nothing had happened.

Military Science consisted of a three-hour session once a week, on the parade ground or indoors, conducted by army personnel as part of the Reserve Officers Training Corps (ROTC) program. Male students were required to complete four semesters of it by the end of their sophomore year.

My toe still hurt when I went to the girls' dorm that night to pick up Ginny Clayborn. Someone had introduced us several days earlier. "Are you going to the get-acquainted dance Friday evening?" I inquired as we were parting.

"I don't know," she replied, a bit hesitantly.

In an uncharacteristic display of courage that both surprised and amazed me, I blurted out, "It might be fun. Could I take you?" Though also surprised, she answered yes and appeared to be pleased.

What will we talk about, I wondered while waiting for her in the dorm lobby. She solved that by asking, as we left, whether it was exciting to live in Lincoln, as I did, and attend a high school where 2,000 were enrolled. Hers, in a town 75 miles away, had less than 200. One advantage of mine, our discussion revealed, was that I knew quite a few of our U of N classmates. She didn't, but had joined a sorority and expected to make friends through it.

Ginny's cheerful enthusiasm impressed me. She was a good conversationalist and a good listener. Her eyes sparkled when she smiled. I enjoyed our evening together and hoped we could have more dates. Unfortunately, it was not to be; those sparkling eyes charmed others, who telephoned well in advance instead of at the last minute. After hearing, "I'm sorry, Bill," again and again, I gave up.

Our paths crossed occasionally the following year. She was "going steady" with a guy named Burton but we sometimes had a

Coke at the Student Union or sat on the steps of Morrill Hall and visited about life in general.

In the spring of 1940, when selecting courses to take as a junior, I gave no thought to registering for additional ROTC. England and France had declared war against Germany the previous autumn, but Europe was far away and it appeared unlikely that America would be drawn into the fighting. By the following spring, however, things had changed. Under the Selective Service Act, I might be required to spend 12 months in the armed forces. Four semesters of Advanced Military Science — one three-hour class weekly — would enable me to do it as an officer instead of as a private. I applied, was accepted, and in the fall of 1941 commenced that phase of my training.

Ginny and I had been dating regularly since she and Burton broke up in April. Another fellow was also courting her. Both of us were serious. If she invited him to her sorority's Christmas dance in mid-December, I would have to decide whether to keep trying or drop out. Elated when the invitation came my way, I considered asking her, the night of the party, to marry me in June. Although I would be in law school for two more years, we could manage financially if she got a job and Dad or another attorney let me work part-time in his office.

My brothers and I usually attended church with our parents on Sunday mornings; but on December 7th, because one brother was in Omaha, the other brother had to participate in a Boy Scout project, and the folks were entertaining friends from Hawaii, I went alone, then proceeded to the law college library and was trying to understand the court's reasoning in a complicated criminal case when voices distracted me. "The Japs have bombed Pearl Harbor," somebody yelled.

Bombed Pearl Harbor? Why? Where's Pearl Harbor? Pushing aside my book, I joined the group crowded around a radio and listened to garbled, ambiguous, inconsistent news reports for half an hour before driving home. Mother and Dad's guests were on the telephone, frantically attempting to reach acquaintances in Honolulu who could obtain information regarding their son, stationed at nearby Hickam Field. The rest of us talked in hushed tones about what had taken place and pondered how we would be affected by President Roosevelt's announcement that our country was at war with Japan. Less than a week later, Germany and Italy declared war against the United States.

My evening with Ginny at the Christmas dance went beautifully and everything seemed perfect when, holding her in my arms afterwards, I whispered, "I love you," and she answered, "I love you, Bill, and have for a long time." I yearned to say, "Will you marry me?" but felt it would be wrong to because my future was so uncertain. Nobody knew what lay ahead for Advanced ROTC cadets – whether they would be sent immediately to reception centers as draftees, to army camps for further training, or to infantry divisions being readied for combat – so the words remained unspoken. Perhaps that's why, when her high school sweetheart showed up early in March wearing the wings of a bombardier, she decided to marry him. It was hard to realize that the war had disrupted things for me so quickly.

The Army Air Corps, Navy, and Marine Corps created programs in which qualified applicants became officers after 90 days of concentrated instruction. I requested permission to withdraw from ROTC and enlist in one of them, hoping this would induce Ginny to change her mind. My request was promptly denied. "You are obligated to complete the course," our colonel declared. "There will be no exceptions."

Most of my close friends graduated at the end of May and entered some branch of the service. I, being in a six-year program – three of pre-law, three of law – remained in college, but as the months crept by grew increasingly lonely. Although I dated now and then, seeking a replacement for Ginny seemed pointless because those finishing their fourth year of Military Science would go to officer candidate schools (OCS) when second semester ended.

In February, 1943, we received orders to report for induction into the army. This, the colonel assured us, was merely a formality. I suspected that it might not be but really didn't care; restless, bored with my classes, embarrassed not to be in uniform like nearly every other young man my age, leaving for OCS right away instead of in June would be fine.

Physical exams were to follow induction. Those who failed them couldn't become officers. That worried a few of the guys but not me. I weighed 165, was five feet eleven inches tall, and except for mild hay fever – precipitated by dust from wheat or straw – had been in good health since outgrowing, at age 13, occasional asthma attacks. "Two doctors examine you," somebody asserted. "One of them peers into your left ear. The second one peers into your right ear. If they don't see each other, you pass."

It wasn't that simple. M.D.'s, nurses and aides went over us thoroughly, after which an orderly asked questions and recorded our answers. When he inquired, "Ever had asthma or hay fever?" I told him no, and hoped God wouldn't punish this dishonesty by causing me to sneeze, choke up, or start wheezing.

My punishment came in a different way. As the final step, a medical officer reviewed each cadet's examination sheet and marked it "Approved" or "Rejected." I walked over to my reviewer and wanted to sink through the floor. It was the doctor who had given me shots for hay fever in high school. "Don't let him remember," I prayed, standing at attention in front of his desk.

He studied my papers, then, slowly looking up, remarked, "Never any asthma or hay fever?" It was a question, not an observation. "No, sir," I replied; having lied once I might as well do it again. His eyes dropped back to the folder. The pendulum of a clock on the wall behind him swung silently back and forth. You could have heard a pin drop as I waited for his decision. Finally, in a low voice, he said, "Very well, you're approved." I tried hard to keep a straight face but smiled ever so slightly. He did too, and winked, then called for the next man.

On April 19th we were ordered to active duty, issued uniforms and directed to move into the university's newly-constructed library building, which had been converted to a barracks. Excited, I rushed home to pick up books, toilet articles and miscellaneous items that might be needed, hurried back to the campus, located my bunk, and at 5 p.m. joined the others for our first formation as full-time soldiers.

Full-time in theory but not in fact, because most of each day we were students. When our sergeant bellowed "everybody up" at

5:50 in the morning, I raced down four flights of stairs to shave and brush my teeth before those less speedy mobbed the 60 or so wash basins that lined the basement walls. We had to be outside by 6:15 for reveille, announcements and, once in awhile, setting-up exercises; eat breakfast at 7; and have beds made, floors swept, and everything in its proper place by 8. From then until 5 we were free to prepare for and attend our regular classes. A half hour of close-order drill at 5 was followed by dinner and study hall, with lights out at 10.

From Saturday noon until Sunday evening we were on our own. I spent that time at home, reviewing for law school finals, working on Military Science assignments, and visiting or playing cards with my parents and brothers. Mike, three years younger than I, would be leaving in July for West Point; David, seven years younger, wasn't old enough to serve in the armed forces. Our family, feeling that the Methodist Church's disapproval of card games was outdated, had played Hearts, Pitch, Black Jack or Fan Tan together on Sunday afternoons since the early 1930's. We also (except for David, who was a sophomore in high school) had beer, wine or a highball on special occasions. Both Mother and Dad took their religion seriously and taught us three boys to follow the golden rule, be kind, and pray regularly for guidance; but abstention from dancing, friendly card games and moderate consumption of alcohol was not part of their creed. Nor, at times, was domestic harmony; they argued frequently, and so did Mike, David and I, but on the whole we were a congenial, happy family.

The officers in charge of our library-based ROTC unit enforced discipline during reveille, retreat, close-order drill and when we marched to the Student Union for meals, but otherwise paid little attention to us. "If this is what the army is like," I mused one afternoon, stretched out on my bunk reading Saint-Exupéry's *Flight To Arras*, "it's going to be an easy life."

It became considerably less easy — for a minute or two — when I had to confront Fred Manley. Each cadet held a "command" position for three days; on this occasion I was platoon leader. We were in formation, at ease but required to stay put. Fred, horsing around, stepped away from the group. I walked over to him and said quietly, "Get back in line, Fred." His facial muscles tightened, his fingers curled into clenched fists. The platoon fell silent. Fred had a temper, and as quarterback of the varsity football team was accustomed to giving orders, not taking them. I expected to end up on the ground with a broken nose or dislocated jaw, but all eyes were on me so backing down was out of the question. Not more than six inches separated our faces as we glared at each other. After what seemed like hours, he turned away and rejoined the formation while I – inwardly – breathed a gigantic sigh of relief.

We were promoted to the rank of corporal and informed that a troop train would transport us, after Commencement, to Fort Leavenworth, Kansas. I bought new sunglasses, got a crew cut that reduced the length of my hair to less than half an inch, and listened attentively when a World War One veteran advised me to "keep your mouth shut, your bowels open, and never volunteer." The morning of May 26th, wearing civilian clothes because our uniforms had been turned in, we marched from the library building to the railway station. A number of parents (including mine) had gathered to say goodbye, but the sergeant in charge made everybody board immediately, so farewells consisted of hasty nods and inconspicuous waves of the hand.

At Leavenworth each of us was issued GI pants, shirts and blouses, work clothes known as "fatigues," socks, shoes, leggings, underwear, neckties, belts, headgear, a field jacket, a raincoat, and dog tags; subjected to vaccinations and inoculations; and overwhelmed with forms relating to allotments, dependents, insurance and war bonds. We were told about chaplains, Special Service officers and the Red Cross, given intelligence and classification tests, taught how to make a bed properly, shown slides depicting the horrible diseases sexual intercourse can lead to, required to memorize the Morse Code, and provided with copies of the Articles of War; then, much to our chagrin, sent back to Lincoln because nobody knew what to do with us. The boys who less than a week before had left to become officers were home again.

During this unanticipated furlough, which lasted almost a month, I played golf, swam, read, hiked along country roads to strengthen my leg muscles, dated girl friends who were still around, and went out with ROTC buddies. One evening four or five of us, drinking beer together, discussed our hopes for the future. Chuck Mason's statement that he expected to be killed in combat surprised me; I'd pictured myself fighting enemy soldiers but hadn't thought about dying.

The next day, recalling our discussion, I considered whether a person beginning his military service ought to keep in mind the possibility of death, then decided that this bridge needn't be crossed until you came to it. I saw the war as a barrier between the present and my future as a happily married young lawyer raising a family in Lincoln. It was up to me to help destroy that barrier.

Orders finally arrived. We returned to Leavenworth, where ROTC graduates from a number of midwestern schools were gathering. I was sitting on my cot, talking to some of them, when an NCO (non-commissioned officer, or "non-com") came in and nabbed several of the group for a clean-up detail. Getting out before he needed additional helpers seemed like a good idea. One by one, half a dozen of us surreptitiously slipped away and headed for the baseball diamond, where behind a dugout wall we discovered that 15 or 20 from our barracks were already there. Learning to goldbrick doesn't take very long.

A couple of days later we went by train to a section of Fort Riley, Kansas, called Camp Funston. The wood-frame huts that lined our company streets weren't much to look at, but they had sturdy double-deck bunks with new mattresses on them. Each hut slept six men. In our latrine building, two of the five stools were marked, "For Venereals Only." You're really in the army now, I commented to myself.

The first few days, while we waited for cadets from other universities, were spent fixing up the place. I helped dig drainage ditches, washed walls, pulled "acres of weeds," resisted the temptation to volunteer when a request for someone to act as company clerk was posted, and on k.p., according to my first letter home, "scrubbed all the garbage cans in Kansas."

This camp for ROTC graduates just opened and is another army experiment. It's the only one in the country. There are 12 officers (all former ROTC instructors, I think) in charge, and about that many non-coms. We are to receive training in weapons, and

> *also physical hardening, and will keep at it until the last men have been shipped to OCS. . . .*
>
> *From the looks of the schedule it's going to be a busy summer. We get up at 5:45, have reveille at 6, start in at 7:15, and except for 50 minutes off to eat at noon continue until 4:30. Dinner at 5, then study hall until 10. We finish at 3 p.m. on Saturdays and apparently are free until 10 p.m. Sundays.*

I wrote the following week that my company had

> *worked with machine guns and grenades, learned about guard duty, and practiced map reading. We have an hour a day of physical training. Took a 5-mile hike yesterday afternoon which included running up a steep hill twice.*
>
> *I signed the payroll so I'll soon be flush with money. Was given a tetanus shot that hurt for only 10 minutes – not bad at all.*

"It's hot and humid but cools off at night," a subsequent letter stated. "They issue us three salt tablets each morning because of the heat. The bugs (mosquitoes, mainly) are terrible." So was the dust that rose from our parade ground during marches, drill or calesthenics; but not until after my departure did I disclose to Mother and Dad that it "made breathing difficult at times." The week had been "toughening," I noted, "though not really hard, and for the most part I enjoyed it a lot."

In "preliminary marksmanship" we fired .22 caliber rifles at targets 50 feet away. My scores were bad. That bothered me. I'd used .22's on the university's indoor range and shot rabbits with them in rural areas near Lincoln. Why had I done so poorly here?

Next came instruction in use of the M-1 rifle, an infantry soldier's basic weapon. Powerful, accurate, dependable, it held a clip of eight cartridges that could be fired one after the other without pausing to recock or reload. We devoted three days to fundamentals — positions, breathing, sighting, trigger squeeze — before marching to a range for practice firing. An NCO demonstrated; it looked easy. The targets, though 500 feet away, were big, and people in pits beneath them raised markers to show where each bullet hit. When it was my turn I did what we'd been taught: wrapped the leather sling around my arm, assumed the prone position, adjusted for windage and elevation, got the correct sight picture, inhaled deeply, and held my breath while slowly squeezing the trigger. A loud roar was followed by intense pain; the right side of my head felt like a horse had kicked it. Because I'd failed to hold the rifle firmly enough, its recoil threw the butt plate into my face. The muzzle, which should be pointing at the target, pointed instead to a cloud drifting lazily across the sky. Mortified, I glanced about and was grateful that nobody appeared to have seen what happened.

I kept it against my shoulder from then on, but ended up in the bottom half when we finished the practice rounds. Zeroing in, breathing and trigger squeeze were no trouble, and I could fire without flinching. My problem was with the barrel; it wobbled enough to make me miss the bullseye and spray the target. I resolved to do better and spent numerous evenings on the parade ground, sometimes with others, sometimes alone, aiming an unloaded M-1 rifle in the prone, sitting, kneeling and standing positions.

"We were on the range all day, starting at 6:45," my next letter reported:

> *The guys who scored well in practice are firing "for record"; the rest of us handle the targets. We marched home under a blazing sun – up hills, across streams, etc., and at practically double time. Many of the boys dropped back and several of them passed out. As a matter of fact 16 were taken to the hospital . . .*

That weekend what began as a prank led to an unpleasant situation. Max Fredricks put some rocks in my bed. Retaliating, I reversed the snapshots and photographs on his shelf so they faced the wall. Later, each of us counter-retaliated. The finale came when he ran off with my barracks bag and I, in pursuit, tackled him where a load of cinders had been dumped. He landed on them, bruising his hands and knees and perhaps his ego. I apologized and tried to help him up. He wouldn't let me, and grabbing my arm yanked me to the ground. We scuffled but were smart enough not to start slugging each other (which could have ended our eligibility for OCS) and soon became friends again.

Going to a movie at the post theater on Saturday evening or

Sunday involved riding in a crowded bus, and the PX adjoining it was jammed, so most of us usually stayed near our own area. I went to Junction City twice, with others, but found it pretty dull.

On guard duty one night my assignment was to walk along a chain-link fence surrounding a storage building. The remoteness of the area gave rise to uneasiness and I recalled how, as a boy, taking my bicycle through the darkness to put it in an unlighted garage behind our house produced this feeling. I wasn't afraid of the dark, just "leery" of it because you didn't know who might be hiding nearby or sneaking forward.

Someone approached; pointing my weapon, I challenged him. It turned out to be a sergeant who was either lost or testing me; I couldn't tell which. He departed. What should I do if attacked? Nobody had mentioned that, or disclosed whether the building contained anything important.

An opportunity to fire the M-1 for record finally arrived. The day was perfect: cool, calm and clear. I hoped my hours of practicing would pay off. They did; in each of the four positions I scored higher than necessary for Marksman and qualified as an Expert. Nothing, at that moment, could have brought greater happiness.

Orders directing us to leave for OCS the following week were accompanied by 36-hour passes. Lee Carswell offered me a ride home. I accepted but almost didn't get away. A non-com who wanted workers started toward my hut. Seeing him, I removed the screen from its rear window, jumped out and ran to where Lee's wife was waiting with their car. We reached Lincoln a few hours later and were back at Riley before Sunday night curfew.

The troop train that carried us to Fort Benning, Georgia, was hot and dirty but had sleeping facilities. I read mystery stories, participated in card games and bull sessions, bought snacks whenever possible to supplement the meals we were served from an improvised kitchen car, and one evening thought about the three and a half months that had gone by since activation of our ROTC unit on April 19th.

They had been, on the whole, neither difficult nor demanding. The lack of privacy that resulted from sharing a room in the library building with dozens of other guys didn't bother me, nor did the regimentation inherent in reveille at 6:15, breakfast at 7, drill at 5, retreat at 5:30, dinner at 6, lights out at 10. Funston wasn't as much fun, due to k. p., parades, physical training, marches, hot weather and those pesky mosquitoes, but we'd been well-treated there by officers and NCO's who believed that college graduates with four years of ROTC needn't be dealt with as if they were new recruits. It felt good to be in uniform, preparing for a role in the world-wide war against German and Japanese aggression that virtually every American wholeheartedly supported.

It had not been that way before Pearl Harbor, when a majority of our citizens were isolationists, adamantly opposed to involvement in foreign conflicts. A report I prepared for my high school Modern Problems class urged students everywhere to "honor those who advocate peace rather than military leaders," and realize that "combat seldom accomplishes its purposes." A paper written in college said: "War is a terrible thing, a tremendous blot on the pages civilization has written. The human suffering it creates is incalculable, its destruction of national wealth is stupendous, the cost in human lives is immeasurable. Surely there is something we can do that will make it possible for men to live in peace." Those feelings hadn't changed, but the situation was now completely different.

Switch engines marked "U. S. Army" pulled our railroad cars through one of Benning's many entrances. In the distance, parachutes with soldiers dangling below them were dropping from the outstretched arms of steel towers. The 17-week course which would lead to my being commissioned a 2nd lieutenant was about to begin. I planned to transfer from Infantry to Air Corps after finishing OCS and become a fighter pilot. That I might someday be a P.O.W. never entered my mind.

2

"Processing" took several days, following which 200 from the Fort Riley contingent and elsewhere departed to start their training. I watched enviously as they marched away.

On August 14th, 183 of us were sent to 3rd Company. After receiving "a multitude of instructions," we were issued rifles, equipment and 58 field manuals ("with more to come"), ran the obstacle course, and met our Tactical Officers. Mine, I wrote the folks, "is a tough cookie who looks like he didn't get past 8th grade." Each Tac supervised a platoon of approximately 45 OC's (Officer Candidates). "No matter where I am or what I'm doing," my letter stated, "he's close by, keeping an eye on me." That, however, wasn't entirely true; Tacs didn't live in our barracks and weren't around in the evenings or on Sundays.

> *The food is excellent. . . . You sit down at tables and help yourself, family style . . .*
>
> *It's hot during the day (also humid) but cool at night. Yesterday there was a sand storm, probably ordered by T. I. S. (The Infantry School) to accustom us to desert fighting . . .*
>
> *We get up at 6:30, stand reveille at 6:45, and are busy from 8:15 to 6:15, with an hour and a quarter off at noon. Supper at 6:30, study hall from 7 to 9, lights out at 10.*

"We've had physical training from 5:15 to 6:15 every afternoon," my next letter noted. "I've managed to stick with it each time, but lots of the fellows weren't able to."

> *Otherwise, it's been all classroom work. Our instructors are capable and experienced men who know their subject from beginning to end and put it across in an interesting way. We're concentrating on aerial photograph reading now, but also studying identification of aircraft, regimental supply systems, and training methods. If it wasn't for the Tac officers, life would be wonderful here. My Tac has eyes all over him. I try to stay on the ball, but it seems like "Stevens, do this" or "Stevens, don't do that" is always ringing out. Today I apparently twisted my body a little in a p. t. exercise, and he really gave me unmitigated hell. "Failure to perform as instructed is insubordination," he warned. My only consolation is that the same thing is happening to the other OC's. It seems like I'm yelled at most, but I suppose the others think they are.*
>
> *I got a "gig" for not having the top of my pack even with the foot of the bed. It looked even to me. He gigged me yesterday because one of my field manuals wasn't in proper sequence. Some of the boys got 6 or 7. Today I didn't get any.*

Gigs were the bane of our existence. Determined to receive as few of them as possible, I strove for perfection in making my bed, polishing my shoes, folding my clothes, cleaning my rifle, and doing the many other things required of us. The blanket on my cot had to be tucked under the mattress so tightly that a coin tossed on it by the inspecting officer would bounce. I shaved at night, when the wash room wasn't jammed, and therefore had more time in the morning, after helping sweep floors and perform similar chores, to arrange my own stuff.

Somebody acquired a radio. We listened to popular songs, played by disc jockeys, while preparing for the new day and wondered what life was like in the outside world.

Our first "field problem" came the following week. Trucks dropped us off in pairs near an uninhabited area of Benning. A non-com handed each twosome an aerial photograph, pointed to where they were, and instructed them to go from there to a designated spot, then to another place, and end up at a third location. The route assigned my partner and me, according to a letter that weekend, *was over hill and dale through dense woods. We couldn't use the aerial photo for the final segment – only a compass. Contrary to general opinion among civilians, you can't take your compass, let it point north, and follow the arrow. It's easier to go in a circle that way than it is without a compass. We crossed terrain (all woods, though) that even the devil wouldn't claim. The deadline was 12:30; arriving later than that results in an "F." Neither Stenton nor I had a watch. We emerged at the destination, checked in, and asked the time. The answer: 12:28. Not bad, eh?*

Having traveled 6 or 7 miles, I'd have enjoyed a little rest. Instead, after a quick meal they subjected us to the worst period yet of physical training, followed by twice over the obstacle course! All of this on the day Georgia temperatures hit new highs (see the enclosed clipping). Someone must have realized that there's a limit somewhere because we were dismissed at 4:15. I had just settled down on the floor to relax (on the floor to avoid mussing up my bed, which must be perfect until 5 p.m.) when a corporal walked in and started calling names. Ah yes, Stevens was among them. Our indentification pictures were accidentally destroyed, he said, and the lst Sgt decided this would be a good time to re-do them. So much for my two free hours. C'est la guerre.

When we went in for supper a couple of fellows were told that their Tac officer needed to see them right away. That was a tough break because they'd probably get nothing to eat. I had finished only half of my meal when word came for me to report at once to mine. At once seems to mean about five minutes ago around here, especially to a Tac, so I jumped. When I reached the orderly room the boys who had left earlier were still waiting. I announced my presence and was informed that the lieutenant would see me "in a little while." It turned out to be quite a little while – an hour and a half to be exact. Each candidate is interviewed by his Tac during the first month. These interviews are supposed to be chummy — the father and son idea. You can imagine how chummy I felt after waiting on the doorstep for that long and missing part of my dinner. Apparently the lieutenant wasn't feeling any too chummy himself. "Your name is William D. Stevens, born Sept. 3, 1920, etc., etc., etc.," he mumbled, reading from a card. I sat there nodding my head so he'd think I was alert. "Ever been drunk?" Well, that question, coming like a bolt out of the blue, certainly got my attention. I gulped and said perhaps there had been occasions when I'd had more than enough to drink but I didn't believe I'd really been drunk.

"Who were you with, boys or girls, and what were you drinking?" I gave some kind of an answer, and then he asked me if I thought these were silly questions. If it had been anybody else I'd have told him exactly what I thought. Instead I said I really didn't see his point in asking them. His response was that he wanted to know how I spent my spare time. I assured him that I didn't spend it getting drunk. Our conversation continued in this cheery vein until I was dismissed. My opinion of him was definitely not enhanced by our chat. As for his opinion of me, I can only fear the worst. One thing is certain: he's no teetotaler himself. Maybe this will be the tie that binds.

I've done well this week – at least he hasn't had to yell at me. Also, I went all week without any gigs. I didn't have any mistakes on the entrance exam (about a 9th grade test) and got an A on the Map Reading exam we took yesterday. The last three days of next week I'm first sergeant, my first chance to show what I can do as a leader.

Mother had written that there might be "spies" in the barracks – OC's put with us to report on what we said and did. That struck me as far-fetched. "However," my answer commented,

I've never let on that I don't like our Tac, although to date I really dislike him immensely. He does everything he can to make life tough for us. The theory is that we're being trained as combat officers; if we can't handle stress here we won't be able to endure the rigors of battle and still inspire our men. That's the reason for calling us away from dinner and then having us wait, and for the relentlessness of the Tacs. I understand this, but it can be carried too far. . . .

The other Tacs in 3rd Company and those in 8th Company, where most of the Nebraskans were, appeared to be more helpful and have a "human" side to them. Several were ROTC graduates themselves. My Tac made it clear that he had no use for "college boys" and thought they shouldn't be in OCS.

Saturday night Pete Shelton, Tony Sonderini and I had two beers and dinner at the Service Club. We'd known each other at the university. "Our meal was swell: roast pork, potatoes, peas, carrots, fruit salad, iced tea and dessert, all for 55 cents." Some evenings, when study hall ended, the three of us went to the PX for a pint apiece of ice cream.

The following Saturday, a second cousin of mine who was stationed at Benning drove me to Columbus, Georgia, for dinner. "We had steak with all the trimmings and a couple of highballs," I wrote on Sunday, then described my activities prior to that:

> *Monday, after a full day outside, we rode in trucks to a God-forsaken section of the post for our night map problem. Each pair received compass directions to follow. Lights of any kind were prohibited, this being enemy territory. However, our compass dials were visible in the dark. My partner and I spent four horrible hours traveling those two miles. It was wooded all the way. Lots of branches lay on the ground. Vines grew everywhere. Sticker bushes abounded. Thorns poked through my clothes. I fell down often and actually walked straight into trees – you couldn't see your hand in front of your face. Streams had cut deep ravines. Once it lightninged and we found ourselves at the edge of a 10-foot pit. Another time, I was ahead of Stenton (my partner) when all of a sudden I plunged downward – too scared to scream and anyway it was all over in a second.*
>
> *I landed in a gully about 15 feet deep, the wind knocked out of me but otherwise okay. What a sensation! The gully was 3 or 4 feet wide. Its sides were almost straight up and I had to strike matches to see how to get out. Later I noticed something luminous ahead of me. I bent over and realized it was a tremendous snake. I don't know whether the snake moved or not, but I sure did. We reached the destination all right and before one a.m., the deadline, but were two tired and battered OC's.*
>
> *Tuesday we worked with M-1 rifles (Garand) and did some preliminary firing. We also fired the Carbine. It feels just like a B-B gun but really packs a wallop. I scored 91 out of a possible 115, which is fairly good. Thursday we fired the M-1 for record and I again made Expert . . .*
>
> *Friday was spent in the field, doing camouflage and hasty fortifications. We dug foxholes, laid barb-wire, etc. Hard and hot work. Got off early, though. It's rained for about an hour the last few days, but we go right on as if the sun were shining. We fired part of our range qualifications in a downpour – could hardly see the target. . . .*

Many thanks for your words of encouragement. I'll probably re-read them often. Things here aren't always too smooth! If I ever go overseas I'll be a lot farther from home than I am now, but even this seems like a long, long way.

Except for Wednesday and Saturday afternoons, our 4th week was devoted to machine guns. We learned to disassemble and reassemble them, then shot at different kinds of targets:

For anti-aircraft firing we used the light and heavy 30 caliber machine guns and also the powerful big 50 caliber. Most of the time we fired at a sleeve towed behind a plane. Our aim was lousy at first and I would have hated to be that pilot, although the distance between plane and towed sleeve was 600 yards. Then we got to fire at radio-controlled aircraft. They're approximately a third the size of regular pursuit planes and fly at 100 m.p.h. Being one-third the size and traveling at one-third the speed, they present a target similar to what we will actually encounter. We brought two down by hitting the motor or radio, which automatically releases a parachute that keeps them from crashing. It was fun and also good training.

The range was near the paratroop jump area. We saw transports fly by and guys bail out. They filled the sky – quite a sight.

Wednesday afternoon we had a demonstration of a battalion in the attack, put on for a number of OCS companies by soldiers from the 300th Infantry and attached Field Artillery, Air Corps, Chemical and Armored units. We moved from hilltop to hilltop to watch everything that took place. Planes simulated the strafing of defending ground troops; others dropped practice bombs (which make a loud noise and send up smoke, but nothing else). They flew at about 50 feet – I could almost touch them. Then P-41's dropped real bombs on a hillside the enemy supposedly held. Next the artillery cut loose and blasted a hill. We couldn't see their 105's and 155's but heard the shells whizzing by above our heads. Chemical units shot smoke shells to conceal friendly forces that were assembling. When the smoke began to clear, tanks started forward, followed by infantrymen. Machine guns and mortars fired tracers close to them and I think a few bullets bounced off of the tanks.

This afternoon we ran the obstacle course, then had an hour of physical training and close-order drill, an hour of command practice, and a two-hour lecture on logistics.

This week seems to have passed without any serious catastrophes. A gig for dirt on the butt plate of my rifle was the only black mark I'm aware of, but my pal the Tac officer may have put many more in his ever-present notebook. Tomorrow I'll stay in bed until 8:30, then eat breakfast, go to church, read "Time," have dinner at the Service Club with some of the guys, and maybe see a movie.

Our obstacle course had fences to climb over or roll under, rocky areas to traverse, walls to scale, ditches to cross on narrow planks, impediments to dodge or crawl beneath, and culverts to squeeze through, all in less than a certain number of minutes. It was tough — especially when you had to do it with full field equipment — and exhausting.

I read *Time* magazine to determine how the war was progressing. Allied troops had advanced across Sicily and entered the toe of Italy. That sounded good, but the ones at Salerno appeared to be in trouble. The Pacific situation was hard to follow because I didn't know where all those islands were and couldn't understand the divergent roles being played by Army, Navy and Marine Corps land, sea and air forces. There had evidently been heavy losses at Tarawa; who now controlled it was unclear. "We hear a news bulletin (issued by Ft. Benning headquarters) every day," my letter to the family remarked, "so I'm up-to-date on the big stuff."

Mother suggested that I visit Warm Springs some weekend, as several Nebraska OC's from 8th Company had done. "I can't, Mom," I replied,

because we don't have Saturday afternoons free like they do. This is the toughest battalion in the regiment. The OCS schedule requires each company to give its trainees 50 hours off (not counting Sundays) during the 17 weeks. That would make 12 1/2 Saturday afternoons, but instead we get ours on weekday afternoons and must often use this time for dental appointments, cleaning rifles, etc. Even going to Columbus is impractical because we have to be back for study hall at 7. So it's no Warm Springs for me.

"OCS," I commented, responding to one of her inquiries, "is

divided into two distinct parts, the academic and that which pertains to leadership."

> *It's the former, now so highly perfected, that "Life" and "Time" wrote about and all the big shots were here to observe. The latter is where Tac officers come in; they supervise our command and drill practice, walk alongside us in every formation, and when we go into the field to work on tactics will record each man's strong and weak points. . . .*
>
> *The news from the other companies in our battalion is disheartening. In the 2d Company, next door to us and a week ahead, the screening board met yesterday, called 76 candidates before it, and ousted 70. In the 1st Company, two weeks ahead of us, the board bounced 50 more. The mortality rate is high because new officers aren't needed. The battalion Exec told us Tuesday evening that thousands of 2nd lieutenants are sitting on their duffs in replacement centers. The government, he said, has fulfilled its obligation to ROTC graduates by admitting them to OCS and will dismiss those not clearly qualified. In one respect I'm fortunate: most of the casualties have been for low grades on written exams like the "Platoon Leaders Computation Test" we took this morning. It was all math and I assume I passed without any trouble, although two of the questions were tricky. I got a B on my basic machine gun test and had a perfect score on the advanced MG test. Also, those ousted for lack of experience, a favorite excuse with ROTC grads, have in general been younger, usually 20 or under. Being 23, I should have an advantage there. At any rate, I'll learn next Saturday whether or not I can stay until the second board meeting, which is five weeks after the first.*
>
> *My turn as top sergeant went okay. You are rated on confidential forms when you do anything like that. I as 1st Sgt would be rated by the OC serving as company commander, and of course by my Tac officer. I have no idea how I was rated. . . .*
>
> *I wish you wouldn't worry about me. I'm getting plenty to eat, sleep well at night, feel fine, and enjoy our bull sessions after study hall.*

The son of a couple the folks knew died when his fighter plane was shot down. "Do you suppose people will have forgotten, 25 years from now, the guys who were killed, and allow our country to go to war again?" my letter asked. "It hardly seems possible that they could. I'm glad photographs of dead servicemen are being published – this may be what some of our complacent citizens need to see."

The following week we worked with Browning Automatic Rifles, hand grenades and bayonets. I liked the BAR but not the hand to hand fighting that bayonet training involved. Trying to kill an enemy soldier with bullets from a rifle or machine gun or shrapnel from mortar shells and grenades didn't bother me. Trying to kill him with a bayonet or trench knife did; it was too intimate, too personal. Lying on the ground during one of our ten-minute breaks, I recalled the boxing lessons Dad had me sign up for at age eleven.

Because I was shorter and skinnier than most 6th grade boys, he felt that knowing how to use my fists properly would help me in encounters with junior high school bullies. When a few of my friends registered for classes conducted by a professional boxer, I did too and was paired with a kid my size. We banged away at each other but neither of us enjoyed it. Physical contact seemed okay in sandlot football, which was played (tackle, not touch) without helmets, shoulder pads or similar equipment; physical contact for the sole purpose of hurting someone seemed wrong.

Well, I was no longer a 6th grader, and if I ever came face to face with an enemy soldier it would be him or me, so when our break ended I aggressively attacked the straw-filled dummies set up to oppose us, and in battling fellow OC's (using sticks with padding on them) did my best to parry their thrusts and strike the fatal blow.

On Saturday the screening board called before it sixty 3rd Company OC's whose performance was considered substandard and discharged over half of them.

Lt. Col. and Mrs. Bradford invited me to dinner. They lived on the post; she was a friend of mother's. Those of us not summoned by the board didn't get back to the barracks until 6, but I managed to reach their quarters by the appointed hour. My haste turned out to be unnecessary; the host wasn't home yet and only one other guest had arrived, a captain attached to The Infantry

School. Mrs. Bradford gave each of us a Martini; while she worked in the kitchen, he and I talked about OCS. "Hoot" Bradford and two lieutenants showed up soon after that. Nobody appeared to be bothered by the fact that a lowly OC was drinking Martinis with a bunch of officers as if he were their bosom buddy.

We had several, and wine with dinner. Later, sitting on a davenport in the living room, I fell sound asleep. Mrs. Bradford laughed when my eyes opened. "Forget it," she said; "Hoot's upstairs getting ready for bed and the rest have gone." In the front yard, under some shrubs, I saw one of the lieutenants, passed out. It seemed inappropriate to disturb him, so I hurried on.

Monday we studied the fundamentals of tactics. Tuesday we rode to a bivouac area, pitched tents, and that night watched patrolling demonstrations until 11:15. Wednesday we were instructed to make our way, after dark, in groups of four, through hostile territory without being caught.

> *The enemy fired machine guns over our heads and used flares, fire-crackers and "grenades" (small paper sacks full of flour). We crawled by a sentry on our stomachs. He knew we were close but couldn't see us because of the high grass. . . .*
>
> *Thursday evening was free. However, rifle cleaning and preparation for a graded test on Friday kept me busy.*

Our 8th week was spent learning about and firing mortars. Saturday Pete Shelton and I had a couple of beers at the PX, then visited 8th Company. "Gosh but things are swell for them," I wrote the folks. "Their Tac is a nice fellow and very helpful." Sunday afternoon, on the steps of our deserted mess hall, Pete told me he was failing in "command" – the ability to give orders clearly, crisply, and with assurance – and wouldn't last much longer as an OC. His voice didn't carry and lacked authority. I tried, without success, to encourage him. Tony had the same problem but remained optimistically hopeful. Fortunately, I was doing well in "command."

Our days in the field were different from those in the classroom. The kitchen crew brought lunch to us and training ended at 5 instead of 6:15. The instant it was over I raced to the trucks in order to sit on a bench rather than the floor. In the company area, sweaty, dirty and weary, we lined up by platoons for announcements from the First Sergeant. After that, some of us ran the obstacle course once or twice to impress our Tacs, then trudged back to the barracks. Exhausted, I relaxed on my cot for a few minutes before stripping off my clothes and ambling into the washroom, where four or five OC's shared each shower head; and after putting on a clean uniform, stood in the chow line with Pete, Tony or other friends until the mess hall opened. Most of us didn't go to Columbus Saturday evenings because the busses were crowded and the number of Benning enlisted men who were either drunk or sick made the ride home unpleasant.

The following week we worked on anti-tank guns and had a night patrolling problem in groups of six:

> *They let us study a map of enemy-held territory for 30 minutes. Then, relying on memory, compasses and (in theory, at least) our splendid training at T. I. S., we had to infiltrate the enemy position to determine where his outposts were, how many occupants and what kind of weapons each had, and whether anybody occupied some buildings. A member of our patrol was captured when he wandered into a three-man outpost. Machine guns fired blanks at us but we managed, by taking advantage of trees, stumps and tall grass, to get away before they spotted our exact location. When we tried to approach the supposedly abandoned buildings, we encountered what sounded like Clark's 5th Army, judging by the rifle fire that came from them. Stimbert crawled forward to investigate. He said a platoon was there (40 men), so we included that in our report. Actually it was only two men, firing from different places to fool us.*
>
> *The problem ended at 3:30 a.m. We returned to the company area at 4:30, had French toast, oatmeal and coffee for breakfast, went to bed at 5:15, slept until 11, and were free in the afternoon.*

The U.S.O. arranged a dance for our company in Columbus. We got there late because the truck drivers misunderstood the address, but it didn't matter — the girls arrived even later. Eight or ten of us slipped out for a highball while we waited for them, then came back. The gal who latched on to me was dull as dishwater; I finally ditched her and sneaked off with two other OC's for another drink. We wanted to have a third one but decided that this might not be wise.

Monday we used 37 mm. and 57 mm. anti-tank guns against moving dummy tanks. "I scored two hits, which is not bad for a beginner," my letter to the family remarked.

The 57 is certainly a powerhouse; you realize it in a big way when, kneeling, you press the trigger. Tuesday we learned about bazookas and anti-tank grenades. Wednesday we had the afternoon and evening off. Pete, Tony and I hitched a ride into town, walked around awhile, and at 3:30 headed for the Waverly Hotel bar. We stayed there until 5, chatting leisurely over drinks (two apiece), then had a marvelous dinner at a different hotel. Home via the bus, got ready for the next day, and hit the hay at 10. This probably doesn't sound very great to you, but it was wonderful to relax in peaceful, quiet, uncrowded surroundings.

Thursday we worked on demolitions and had a lot of fun – just like a bunch of little kids. We blew up a railroad tie and blasted a couple of steel rails and a tree stump with TNT and used a bangalore torpedo to destroy barbed wire entanglements. Friday was spent on booby traps and anti-personnel mines. Our group set traps (unarmed) for the fellows in another group and they set traps for us. We also laid a mine field and cleared one laid by somebody else, using detectors part of the time and prodding with our bayonets the remainder of the time. Today we built roadblocks and hid booby traps around them.

That weekend each OC received sheets on which to rank and "evaluate" the other members of his squad. We'd done this once before – because, our C.O. [Commanding Officer] explained, "leaders must be able to size up those serving under them." The true reason, I suspected, was to reveal shortcomings he and the Tacs hadn't noticed. Making us rank one another seemed even worse; that was their job, not ours. However, the sheets were explicit: "Rate the best man in your squad #1, the next best #2, and so on. Comment on the strong and weak points of each. Do not rate or comment on yourself." I felt like a stool pigeon, since most of the guys in my squad were excellent OC's, highly qualified to become 2nd lieutenants. The rest, though not outstanding, were more qualified than our Tac. Since I clearly couldn't say that,

I emphasized their strengths and mentioned only obvious weaknesses.

A captain just back from North Africa taught us things about combat that weren't in our books and hadn't been covered by our instructors. After that we spent a little time on 105 mm. howitzers, "biggest of the infantry weapons," then started "in earnest" on tactics, which, I wrote Mother and Dad,

> *is interesting but darn hard. So far we've worked primarily on tactics of the individual soldier and of rifle platoons – how they can most effectively advance against enemy forces over various types of terrain. It's too complicated to describe in a letter, so I won't try. We also worked on tactics of weapons platoons and practiced defensive tactics. The latter included being run over by hostile tanks while in foxholes – it was really nothing at all, just a little dirt on the back of my neck – and having real mortar barrages laid down a couple of hundred yards in front of us.*
>
> *The boys who aren't doing well are beginning to feel it now. They get the tough assignments as student leaders in drill and during tactics exercises. This puts plenty of pressure on them. One of the guys in my barracks was company commander last week and is scheduled to be platoon sergeant tomorrow and platoon leader next week. I haven't had any of those jobs lately, just a private in the ranks, which is the best place in the world to be when you're an OC.*
>
> *A meeting of the battalion screening board is scheduled for Friday. I don't think there's much chance of my being called before them. It's nice to feel a bit more confident, but that doesn't change my opinion about 3rd Company. We're still treated like prisoners. Almost everyone speaks of his barracks as his cell, and the description is often appropriate. None of us will regret leaving, in spite of the fact that our work has been tremendously interesting and our instructors excellent. It shows how a few officers can convert something that ought to be good into something unpleasant.*
>
> *I doubt if you realize how much letters mean to us, especially letters from home. We get lonesome now and then, and at times discouraged. Hearing what you've been doing and news about my friends makes a world of difference.*

The board meeting resulted in Tony and six or seven others being dismissed from OCS. They were sent to Casual Company for assignment to replacement centers. Another man was set back five weeks. This brought to over 40 the number ousted for unacceptable grades on written examinations, poor attitude, lack of command ability, or deficient performance in the field.

The following week we hiked to a bivouac area, pitched our tents, and resumed tactics instruction, which included "marching several miles, double-timing several more"; crossing a chasm on rope bridges put up by the engineers, then hand over hand on a single rope; crawling through a field where .30 caliber machine guns shot live ammunition 18 inches above our heads while soldiers hidden behind trees threw firecrackers at us and detonated buried explosives to simulate bursting shells. This gave us experience in advancing under fire. Then, to gain experience in firing from the hip at unexpected targets when there isn't time to assume one of the four basic positions and take aim, we ran across a hill where concealed cardboard riflemen unexpectedly popped up. Wednesday we were awakened at four in the morning to defend against advancing troops. I was assigned to an anti-tank squad. Five of us "had to push the 37 mm. gun, which weighs 912 lbs., over hill and dale." Thursday we arose at 2:30 for a dawn attack:

> *This time I had it easy because we used a three-quarter-ton truck to pull the gun and I rode everywhere. From our initial location on top of a high hill we had a swell view of the enemy position on which our artillery and mortars were dropping shells and over which tracers from machine guns were making weird patterns. It was impressive.*
>
> *Saturday we took the Army Ground Forces Physical Fitness Test. It consists of five parts: (1) Pushups – 3% given for each; I did 34, thereby getting 100%. (2) Burpees – 9% for each, with a 20-second time limit; I did 11, got 99%. (3) Agility – run 10 yards, crawl 10 yards on belly, run 10 yards, creep 10 yards on hands and knees, run 10 yards, hop 10 yards with both feet together, then run 10 more yards. Time limit, 30 seconds. I did it in 24. (4) Piggy back – run 75 yards with a person on your back; time limit, 20 seconds. I did it in 17. (5) run 300 yards across rough terrain, deduct 4% for each second over 45. I did it in 47 for 92%. So I passed easily, as did most of the others.*

That weekend we again received sheets on which to write about and rate fellow squad members. There were now only ten in mine, Tony and two others having been bounced. "Be careful what you say," our Tac warned. "Go easy on negative statements. Don't carelessly use words that might hurt somebody." He hadn't told us this the previous two times. Stenton, whose cot was next to mine, asked me that night whether the Tac's remarks would make any difference in what I wrote. "Probably," I replied; "What do you suppose he meant?" Svoboda heard us talking and came over; before long, the entire squad was present, discussing this final evaluation. Stimbert said a Tac officer in 8th Company advised his OC's not to bring up weaknesses at all. Convinced that adverse comments on previous sheets contributed to Tony's downfall, I mentioned that omitting them seemed like a good idea. A couple of others felt that way too. A few didn't say what they thought. No one openly disagreed. I spent Sunday preparing my rankings and describing each man's strengths.

"The pressure is really on now – things are moving fast and furiously," I wrote the folks the evening of November 27th:

> *Our Thanksgiving dinner was marvelous. We were in the field all day, but by cutting our lunch time to 20 minutes finished at 4:30. We had turkey, mashed potatoes, corn, peas, rice, combination salad, fruit cocktail, cranberry sauce, hot rolls and butter, pumpkin pie, ice cream, cookies, and cake. My stomach bulged. After dinner some of the boys sang and played the piano and put on skits. Even our officers (who brought their wives) enjoyed it.*
>
> *We got up at 2:30 a.m. Friday to practice troop movements and kept at it all day. Up at 3:15 a.m. Saturday for a night advance and dawn attack on a village. The village was Benning's famed "Heineberg," which you saw pictures of in "Life" last May. It would have been fun if everyone hadn't been so damn tired. We finished the attack at 8:30, took a graded test and were busy until 6 p.m.*

I didn't disclose in this letter the difficulties my squad had encountered in connection with our rating sheets, but in a long one written over the following week and a half described in detail what happened after we handed them in on Monday morning, November 22nd:

> *That afternoon, all ten of us were ordered to report to Capt.*

Coppel, C.O. of our company. He called us into his office alphabetically. Our Tac was sitting beside him and did the talking. "These rating sheets are not acceptable," he said; "You will prepare new ones and deliver them to me at 0700 tomorrow. Your comments must indicate who is the top man and who is lowest." The others were told the same thing.

In a bull session that night the majority felt we should stick to what we'd previously written. "They're trying to trick us," someone suggested. "If we change, the captain will claim sufficient thought wasn't given to them the first time." I disagreed, but acknowledged that this might be true. Swanson, who is last alphabetically, said Lt. Koenig (our Tac) left the orderly room right after he (Swanson) did. "Nobody else was around so I asked him whether the statement about going easy on weaknesses still applied. He turned his back on me and walked away."

I revised my comments, pointing out in them which men excelled in command ability, tactical expertise, inspiring confidence, developing esprit de corps, and the like, and which were less skilled in these respects, hoping this would make it clear who was first and who was at the bottom.

Tuesday afternoon the C. O. sent for Svoboda and gave him hell for reversing the 6th and 7th men in his rankings. I breathed a sigh of relief; I'd kept a record and knew mine were the same. My relief was short-lived; the remaining nine of us were summoned a few minutes later. Most of the others got criticized for changing something. This, the captain declared, showed that their initial sheets were either a lie or poor judgment. All he told me, however, was that my evaluations didn't adequately reveal which men were the best and which the worst.

So we spent another evening (having missed dinner two nights in a row) preparing new sheets. In these I discussed weaknesses as well as strengths. I was writing in the latrine (because lights were out in the barracks) when Stimbert came in. "I've just been interviewed by the battalion exec (executive officer)," he announced, "who stated in no uncertain terms that we were dishonest in not mentioning the unfavorable as well as the favorable things, that T.I.S. is not commissioning dishonest OC's, and that each of us might as well kiss our commissions goodbye." "He's trying to scare you," I replied; "We're not dishonest and they aren't going to dump ten of their best men." But after talking to him awhile longer, I wasn't so sure. . . .

When we returned from the field Wednesday the captain said, "The following candidates will report to me at once." Here we go again, I whispered to Stenton, but he named only 4 of the 10 and I wasn't one of them. Their latest sheets were unsatisfactory and must be re-done.

We went out at 3 a.m. Friday and got back to the company area around 9 a.m. Again a list of names was read; it included the bottom four in my rankings and quite a few from other platoons. "These candidates will change to 'A' uniforms and appear alphabetically before the screening board, starting immediately." It looks like I'm okay, I thought, and relaxed for the first time all week, but my joy soon vanished; a "supplemental" list named all ten of us. So we traipsed over to the orderly room and there I sat for three hours while one by one those ahead of me were called in.

My turn came at 12:30. The board consisted of Colonel Orton (Director of Training for OC's), our battalion C.O. and our company commander. They were seated behind a table; my Tac officer was at the end of it with a notebook. "You have a fine record," Col. Orton told me. He picked up my rating sheets and read what I'd written regarding my #1 man. "That's an excellent estimate of this candidate, Stevens; far superior to the tripe we often get in these evaluations." Then he read the comment about my last man. "You weren't fooling anybody with this. Why didn't you discuss his shortcomings?" My answer was that if I wrote about them, those who weren't acquainted with the candidate would tend to lay hold of the faults and overlook the good, and since my total analysis of each candidate was that his strengths exceeded his weaknesses, I didn't want this to occur. "You used poor judgment, which indicates inablity to arrive at sound decisions," the colonel declared, "and appear to have participated in a dishonest agreement. I'm submitting this to the full T.I.S. board for review and consider it unlikely that you will be commissioned." I left there 99% convinced that all ten of us were through as OC's.

99%, perhaps, but not 100%; I just couldn't believe they would kick us out. That's why, after bringing it up to date, I didn't mail my long letter to the folks. It seemed foolish to worry them when, in the end, everything would be all right. We hadn't agreed not to comment on weaknesses; but even if we had, that wouldn't justify dismissing us.

Grounds for dismissal definitely existed, however, if agreement of some kind was reached and we attempted to conceal it by lying. Was I wrong in feeling that the discussion around my cot didn't result in an understanding – the equivalent of agreement – that only positive statements would be made?

"Smitty," I said, walking over to Harlan Smith, who had been highest in my ratings each time, "is it true that the guys in the squad agreed not to say anything bad about each other on our rating sheets?"

"Hell, no," he replied. "We were only trying to figure out what Koenig wanted us to do."

Reassured, I pondered whether not referring to weaknesses indicated poor judgment and inability to arrive at sound decisions. Did the Tac's remarks, coupled with his refusal to clarify them, plus what we learned from an adjacent company, supersede the rating sheets' unequivocal, Comment on the strong and weak points of each? My conclusion, after much thought and a serious effort to view it objectively, was yes: our Tac, having no authority to countermand this instruction, wanted us to know that it shouldn't be followed. If he'd been man enough to admit that he told us to "go easy," and turned his back when asked by Swanson whether that still applied, maybe none of this would have happened.

Saturday evening Slaybaugh asked me to have a Coke with him at the PX. "Bill," he said when we were alone, "somebody in our squad told Colonel Orton the ten of us agreed not to mention shortcomings."

"He's wrong," I replied, "but I guess each person has a right to his own opinion."

"It wasn't an expression of opinion, Bill. He went to Orton voluntarily, on his own, in order to get the rest of us in trouble."

"Why? That doesn't make sense, Dan."

"It might. I think one of the guys we ranked low did it to get even."

When I asked how he knew somebody went to Orton, he answered: "My brother's best friend works in Orton's office. He heard them discussing it. Orton said we wouldn't get away with such dishonesty on his watch."

"The T.I.S. board won't believe one guy when nine others say the opposite."

"You're wrong, Bill. Orton believes the one guy. The rest will do what he says."

Lying in bed that night I pondered whether this could be true.

Sunday afternoon several of us went to a movie. When we got back to the barracks, Simpson greeted us with unpleasant news. He had gone to see the colonel in charge of ROTC at his university, who was now at Benning and (my long letter home explained), "on the T.I.S. board."

> *Apparently eager to obtain evidence of our alleged cheating, he brought in two other officers who are board members. They questioned Simpson until, worn down and confused, he acknowledged that there was a meeting at which we "might have" agreed not to write negative statements about each other. He had to draw a diagram showing where the meeting took place. When they asked him who the leader was, he answered, "Nobody."*
>
> *It made me mad that these officers would do this to a fellow who innocently and in good faith went to one of them for advice. I wished they could understand that it was a bull session such as we've had many times, not a meeting; that all we did was express opinions regarding our Tac's remark; and that we hadn't agreed to anything. Maybe I filled out those first sheets improperly, but I didn't do it that way because of any implied, expressed or "gentleman's" agreement.*
>
> *The next day the ten of us (and others) were ordered to appear before the full T.I.S. board at 1 p.m.. I was determined to tell them the facts, and not leave until they let me, but they spent all afternoon with three OC's from 3rd platoon and didn't reach our group until chow time. Then they called a low man instead of Simpson, who is first alphabetically. I was fed up with this and decided not to miss another meal, so I ate dinner while the rest of them sat around waiting.*

The second man taken from our group was also low on my list. Then, about 8 p.m., they called me. I reported and sat down facing Col. Orton, two other colonels, and two Lt. Colonels, one of the latter being our Bn. C.O. Also present were my Tac officer, our company commander, and the battalion executive officer. They kept me there an hour and a half and I never got such a grilling in my life. But I was relaxed and not afraid. I knew I hadn't participated in a dishonest deal even though they thought I had. I tried my hardest to convince them but realized when I left that they didn't believe me.

Col. Orton said I was the natural leader of the group, and since the meeting took place by my cot and I advised the others to be extremely careful about what they wrote, the board's conclusion was that everybody else got the idea from me and that I knew they were going to fill out their sheets as they did. I told him I didn't "advise" anybody to do anything but simply participated in the discussion and didn't know the rest were ignoring faults and learned later on that their reason for not mentioning them wasn't the same as my reason; also that there were too many capable, intelligent men in our squad for me to be considered the only leader. The Bn. C.O. confirmed that the reason I gave for not listing faults wasn't the same as that given by the rest. They asked me some of those questions six times, trying to get the answer they wanted.

This morning the ten of us, along with numerous others, were ordered to appear before the board. It's in session now, taking OC's one by one, bouncing some, okaying some. None of our group has been called yet. Only three of us have faced the full board. Those who haven't may succumb to their third-degree methods. I'm not fooling myself; my life in T.I.S. hangs by a slim, slim thread. I wouldn't give myself one chance in fifty. But because there is still that chance, and because hope springs eternal, I won't say I'm through.

* * *

Now, however, it's a different story, for I am indeed through and have already talked with you three times on the telephone.

To make this complete I'll carry on from where I left off yesterday. They didn't get to me until afternoon. The session lasted an hour and again they grilled me plenty. I fought hard but their minds were made up. All ten of us and 28 others were notified of our dismissal from OCS. I realize that I brought it on myself, but the punishment does seem a little stiff. Shelton, who's not in my squad, was bounced for unsatisfactory performance in the field.

I don't intend to go overseas as a corporal, though what other choices there are is uncertain. It's almost impossible (without pull) to become an aviation cadet after you've had this much infantry training.

Don't worry about me; I can take it. This isn't the first injustice the world has ever seen.

Walking dejectedly to the PX, I felt sorrier for Mother and Dad than for myself. Because I hadn't mailed the long letter or mentioned in those I sent that we were in trouble, my phone call caught them unawares and they were crushed.

A telegram arrived that evening:

Regret to inform you that your son was relieved from the Infantry Officer Candidate School for a flagrant violation of instructions relating to the manner and procedure in rating other candidates. His case along with those in collusion with him was carefully investigated by a faculty board of senior officers who recommended that they be dismissed. I have personally examined these cases and have approved the findings and recommend-ations of the board. Bonesteel, Commandant, The Infantry School.

Dismissing us had seemed unfair to me. The folks considered it not only unfair but arbitrary, unreasonable and completely unjustified. Dad telephoned Major General Bonesteel to request a rehearing or review. Smith's mother contacted their senators in Washington; she knew them personally because her deceased husband had served as governor.

"Perhaps, Dad," my reply to an understanding note from him said, "I didn't do the right thing in getting into that discussion around my bed, and in what followed, but it was all so apparently innocuous and insignificant."

I feel fine (physically) and am not undone by what's happened, although it's hard not to be a little bitter. What really hurts is that many less qualified guys are being commissioned; some of them are lousy leaders. Don't worry; it will take a lot more than this to destroy me.

Happy Birthday to the best dad in the world.

"A little bitter" was putting it mildly. I was sore as hell and rued the day I signed up for Advanced ROTC. What a stupid decision that had been.

I wrote again on Sunday, December 5th:

> *Unless it appears tomorrow that there's a chance of my getting back into OCS, I expect to start an application for Air Corps on its way. . . .*
>
> *It was swell to talk to you this morning; thanks for your loyal support. I'll be glad when I finally know what's in store for us — living from hour to hour isn't too pleasant. We drill some and run the obstacle course to keep in condition, but that's about the extent of our activities. Can't leave, though, because orders might come.*

Monday afternoon a telegram from Bonesteel notified the folks that a board consisting of a colonel, a lieutenant colonel and two majors would "review and make recommendations on all cases, including your son's." It convened on Tuesday. Three days later, in a lengthy letter, I described what took place:

> *The first witness was Lt. Col. Redfern, our battalion C. O. He did a poor job of testifying, hesitated, hedged in his answers, and I think his testimony, on the whole, helped us more than it hurt us although he certainly didn't intend it to.*
>
> *The next witness was Col. Orton. He is a hard-nosed old buzzard with as icy a stare as you ever saw. His testimony was all against us and he didn't hedge or hesitate in saying what he thought. However, he admitted that his mind was made up before we ever appeared in front of him, which looked like a pretty good point for us.*
>
> *Wednesday morning we started out with Capt. Coppel, our company commander. He really squirmed on the stand and he had good reason to. He never did tell the truth – either hedged or lied. The hedging at least was obvious to the board, for again and again the chairman told him to answer yes or no, or at least give direct answers. He had a hard time squirming out from under some of the questions one major asked, though, and also from under some of ours.*
>
> *Lt. Koenig, our Tac officer, was next. The way he testified confirmed my opinion of him as a mean, narrow-minded individual. He told several out and out lies which were obvious to*

me but may not have been to the board. However, I think they could see from his demeanor that he was lying, or at least not telling the whole truth. . . .

After that, each of us was allowed to make a statement if we wanted to, sworn or unsworn, and then we were asked a few questions. I won't go into the details of my sworn statement, but it was designed to show (1) that discussing rating sheets in a bull session was not contrary to any instructions ever given us, (2) that our absence of unfavorable comments was caused by the Tac officer's remarks and other factors, (3) that our difficulty with subsequent rating sheets resulted from lack of instructions, and that we attempted to obtain instructions and couldn't, (4) that the T.I.S. Board had already reached a decision in its own mind and therefore couldn't be said to have conducted an impartial review, (5) that Lt. Col. Redfern and Capt. Coppel (who with Col. Orton recommended our dismissal orginally) were dominated by Orton. . . .

Yesterday afternoon the special board went into closed session to deliberate on the evidence. . . . They gave us a fair hearing and may believe we got a bum deal, but it's not likely that Bonesteel will reverse what's already been done. . . .

I addressed an envelope, sealed the letter in it, and leaning back, recalled Col. Orton, jaw set, a shiny silver eagle on each shoulder of his blouse, three rows of ribbons above his left pocket, standing erect before that board as he swore to tell the truth. Those steel-blue eyes didn't blink when the chairman said each of us would be allowed to cross-examine him. It must have seemed incredible to a career army officer that something like this could occur. It seemed incredible to me, too.

It also seemed incredible that we had been kicked out for an infraction that wasn't altogether our fault. The many hours we devoted to map and aerial photograph reading, day and night patrolling, hand to hand fighting, bayonets, booby traps, mines, demolitions and tactics; to learning about and firing M-1 rifles, carbines, automatic rifles, 30 and 50 caliber machine guns, 37 and 57 mm. anti-tank guns, mortars, bazookas, grenades, and howitzers; to studying supply systems, communications, training methods, and discipline; to running obstacle courses and enduring without complaint the psychological pressures, criticism, annoyances, discomfort and weariness that OCS involved – had all been in vain.

Friday afternoon we were summoned to hear the decision. Captain Coppel was present and a captain I didn't recognize. It crossed my mind that The Infantry School might be transferring us to another OCS company and he was our new C.O. Before I could consider this possibility a door opened and the members of the special board filed in. The chairman announced that their recommendations to General Bonesteel had been approved by him and an order implementing them issued. "Blessed is he who expects nothing," I whispered silently, preparing myself for disappointment.

The order was almost beyond belief: no failure to follow instructions, no collusion. We were cleared 100% and would graduate with those in our class who remained. None of us cheered or jumped for joy as we rose and saluted, but the smiles on our faces were a mile wide.

Saturday morning I bought the uniforms and insignia an officer was required to have. Back in our old barracks, holding in my hand the gold bars of a 2nd lieutenant, I said to myself with deep feeling, "You earned them."

After a swearing-in ceremony on Monday each graduate received a ten-day delay en route prior to reporting for his next assignment, which for everyone in my squad except Stenton was the 26th Infantry Division, stationed at Camp Campbell, Kentucky. Stenton was sent to an MITC unit; those letters, somebody suggested, stood for "Military Intelligence Training Corps." That surprised me; could Stenton have been a stool pigeon, with this as his reward? Did he make up the story about our agreeing and transmit it to Orton in order to win the MITC appointment? I never did find out.

Although the rating sheet battle diminished my favorable opinion of T. I. S., I felt that our training had been excellent – truly outstanding. Getting a Tac officer who disliked "college boys" was unfortunate – a tough break – but such things happen. In the future, no doubt, there would be lucky breaks.

3

At Lincoln's Army Air Corps base, during my delay en route, I filled out the forms and passed the physical exam required for flight training. My application for transfer, the officer in charge informed me, would have to be submitted at Camp Campbell and from that point on move "through channels."

I went by train to Hopkinsville, Indiana, arrived about 11 p.m., stayed all night in a hotel, and spent the next morning at the railway station waiting for one of my Benning friends to arrive. Reporting for duty would be easier, I felt, if two or more of us did it together. Nobody showed up, so after lunch I boarded a military shuttle bus that let me off in front of an unpretentious building marked, "26th Division Headquarters." Not a soul was in sight.

Uncertain whether hauling my suitcase inside would be proper, I left it by the curb, walked through the door and told a corporal standing behind a desk why I was there. He directed me to Captain Elgar, who thumbed through half a dozen dog-eared files and eventually muttered, "101." This, I discovered, referred to the 101st Infantry Regiment, which sent a jeep to pick me up.

The only officer at its headquarters was a friendly lieutenant named Bosserly. He commented that things were "sort of disorganized" because the division had just returned from a two-week bivouac. Five minutes later the adjutant sauntered in, glanced at my orders, scribbled "E" on a slip of paper, and departed without speaking. What kind of an outfit is this, I wondered.

Bosserly located a bed I could use, took me to supper at the PX, and when we parted stated that I'd been assigned to Company E and should go there in the morning.

I did, and reported to Lieutenant Kaznolwicz, the company commander, who eased my concern by saying, "I'm glad you're here; we need another platoon leader." He asked what training I'd had and told me about the 101st. At noon I met Jud Sikorski, his executive officer, and Lieutenants Dorgan, Gray and Albertson, leaders of E Company's Second, Third and Fourth Platoons. They arranged for me to move in with Gray. "We share a room equipped with two steel cots and nothing else," I wrote the folks:

> *Living in the BOQ (Bachelor Officers Quarters) is great: no rules, no inspections, an orderly to make the beds and clean up (it's the C.O.'s orderly but he takes care of our room too). As I was unpacking, two hours ago, a Lt. walked in, introduced himself, and invited me to come across the hall for a beer. He had a case on ice. Nearby there are several fellows spiking Cokes. Don't get the idea that these guys drink all the time, though; they don't. This is Christmas weekend and everybody is off duty until Sunday afternoon.*
>
> *The 26th (known as YD, for Yankee Division) is a top-notch outfit but definitely not an easy one. They spend two or three weeks a month in the field, engaging in mock warfare to sharpen their skills, leading a harder life here than many men overseas.*

That night I went to the Officers Club with half a dozen lieutenants from the BOQ. The next day, Christmas, almost everyone was gone. I wrote letters to friends and in the evening had a couple of beers and saw a movie with Lt. Kaznolwicz. The other officers called him Kaz, so I did too. He called me Steve.

Monday morning, December 27th, I was introduced to Walter Mahlin, a tech sergeant who had been in charge of First Platoon but now would be second-in-command under me. We talked awhile, then he brought in his assistant, Sgt. Mulvaney, and the platoon's other non-coms, most of whom had joined YD as privates during its National Guard days. They no doubt considered me an inept, ineffective ROTC shavetail. This, to a large extent, was true; I lacked experience and realized that, notwithstanding my thorough training at Benning, directing men who'd been with the regiment for months and knew the ropes would be difficult. Gray gave me helpful hints, and in the weeks ahead I learned a lot from Sgt. Mahlin. Fortunately, being replaced by a brand new 2nd lieutenant didn't bother him and we got along fine.

He was gentle and soft-spoken, affable with our privates, the other NCO's and me, not nasty, petty or temperamental. I didn't know the extent of his formal education but he seemed intelligent and appeared to be a person you could trust. The fact that I was an officer and he wasn't didn't matter to me, as far as the relationship between us was concerned, but it did to him.

A field problem – my first since being commissioned – began that evening. We left after dinner, marched seven miles "through three inches of mud" to a bivouac area, dug foxholes and, wrapped in shelter halves, tried to sleep. Breakfast was at 4:15, following which we marched ten miles, in pouring rain, to an assembly point. There the battalion commander, Major O'Neal, ordered me to have the platoon advance alongside Company F, which would be to our right. We went seven more miles before encountering the enemy. A runner I sent to tell Kaz its resistance was holding us up returned 15 minutes later, unable to find him. Scouting around, I discovered that my platoon, the F Company one we'd been guiding on, and a mortar unit to our rear commanded by Lt. Schmidt, were all alone. Where the rest of the battalion was, nobody knew. I hadn't the slightest idea what to do. Schmidt took charge; we pushed forward and eventually reached the initial objective, where an umpire terminated the problem because the downpour made it impossible to see more than a few feet ahead. Everyone else, he announced, got lost.

On Wednesday, "wading through the mire," I helped conduct a patrolling demonstration. Thursday I supervised carbine firing and assisted with an equipment inspection at regimental headquarters. Friday I lectured on aerial photographs. That evening, as Company Duty Officer, I checked the enlisted men's barracks at 11 o'clock to make sure all of them were there; then lay awake on my cot until the year ended at midnight. What 1944 would bring couldn't even be guessed at. I celebrated its arrival by participating in reveille at 6:30 a.m. with the battalion's other duty officers.

"The social part of life here," my weekend letter home remarked,

> *is generally enjoyable — when the fellows are relaxing they are friendly and cheerful. But during duty hours, and especially on these problems in the field, everybody is under a strain from being tired and cold or from having been chewed out by someone who outranks him, and things aren't so pleasant then.*
>
> *I'm not afraid of hard work, but feel wasted filling a job that doesn't call for anything more than a strong back and vivid vocabulary. I know the Air Corps is neither safe nor easy, but at least the flying officers lead a pretty decent life while they live. My application for flight training is on its way and I'm hoping more than ever that it will go through soon.*
>
> *Won't it be wonderful if the war ends this year!*

Explaining to Kaz my desire to become a pilot had been difficult because I liked him and felt that despite our different backgrounds, he liked me. About 5' 9" tall, he was square-built and solid, pleasant but tough, a street-smart, fearless guy in his late twenties who before joining the army worked in the coal mines of western Pennsylvania. "I can't stop you from applying," he said, "but wish you would stay."

During the first two weeks of January we were in the field twice for combat problems that lasted several days. "I did okay as far as leading my platoon is concerned," a letter to Mike reported, "and am still hitting on all cylinders, but when the war is over I'll never again sleep outdoors." I served as investigating officer for court martials involving AWOL soldiers, did some firing with the M-1 rifle and carbine, and whenever possible stopped at the PX for a chocolate milkshake. A couple of times I had two.

Kaz warned me that one of the company commanders in our battalion was a homosexual who sooner or later would make a pass at me. "Just tell him no, Steve, and he'll leave you alone." The following Saturday I woke up about 1 a.m., aware that somebody was sitting on the edge of my cot. His hand started under the blanket. "Go away," I said in a low but firm voice. He immediately departed. It never happened again and neither of us mentioned the incident when our paths crossed after that.

On January 22nd the division left for central Tennessee to participate with thousands of other troops in "maneuvers," during which opposing forces — the Reds and the Blues — would struggle for success in imaginary battles. There were to be eight problems, one per week, each lasting four or five days. Because we would not be returning to Camp Campbell, officers were allowed to take the footlockers they'd been issued. I put my good clothes in mine, not knowing when, if ever, I would see them again. Major General Paul, YD's commander, had announced that he expected us to go from maneuvers to a staging area and then overseas.

We spent our first week in Tennessee learning to use radios and field telephones for communication, practicing river crossings in assault boats, and getting accustomed to the cold weather. I received special instruction in wire tapping, and one evening was in charge of 70 soldiers who had passes to Lebanon:

> *The taverns were jammed and I'd seen the picture at the town's only theater, so I bought a magazine and read it in the courthouse hospitality room until 10, then went to the MP station to find out if any of our group had been picked up (none were). We got back about midnight.*
>
> *I know all the men in my platoon personally now and I think they like me. Being their leader is no easy job, but I feel as though things are going well – very well in fact. It's such a big job that even a little success seems worthwhile.*
>
> *All of us have blankets drying on ropes or tree branches. Ordinarily we're required to keep them in our tents (which are camouflaged) but today is an exception. The ground is wet but so far not sloppy or muddy.*
>
> *Open-air movies were shown last night – an old Laurel and Hardy film plus a Terry Toon. Also, another load of Milky Ways came in. I bought two dozen.*

The first problem commenced on Monday. Company E and other units of the 101st left the bivouac area in a long line of trucks. About noon Major O'Neal told me to organize a motorized patrol and explore the terrain in front of us. Three jeeps were provided; I set out in them with eight of my men. A mile or two down the road we entered a wooded area. Remembering an OCS training film, I stopped and had scouts go ahead on foot. Nothing happened, so the rest of us started forward. After awhile, still in the woods, I stopped again and, suspicious, sent a group out to reconnoiter. When they didn't return I prepared a message for someone to take to headquarters; then, proceeding cautiously toward sounds of activity, ran into the C.O. of an adjoining battalion. His companies planned to withdraw, he said. I headed back to inform O'Neal but couldn't locate his CP [Command Post]; it had moved and nobody knew where he was. The regiment's Operations Officer advised me to keep looking, so a sergeant and I scoured the area in one of the jeeps. We parked it in a clump of trees, walked through the woods, saw nothing, then couldn't find our jeep. "My God, Lieutenant," the sergeant moaned, "what if we have to pay for the damn thing? We'll be in hock the rest of our lives." That thought had crossed my mind, too, but of greater concern was how I would explain to a board of inquiry that I lost a jeep. We finally spotted it and soon found 2nd Battalion's CP. O'Neal was gone so I reported to his Exec, Captain Bahr, and had just rejoined my platoon when a corporal drove up. "Sir, Captain Bahr wants you to locate the 3rd Battalion Command Post. You can ride with me. He didn't want to go himself because it's too dangerous."

"Well, 2nd lieutenants are expendable," I responded, laughing but inwardly displeased. Captain Bahr, in my opinion, was a jerk.

We went along country roads, not knowing where our troops or the enemy's forces were; and, hoping not to be captured, left the vehicle from time to time to search on foot. Eventually I gave up and reported my lack of success to Bahr. His only comment was, "You should have tried harder."

The problem "kept us on the run," I wrote the folks. "No sleep Monday night and no food Tuesday because Company E's kitchen trucks were captured. It ended Thursday. We pitched tents, had a hot meal, and on Friday rested."

I'm in command of the battalion's wire-tapping team and have available for use, if sent behind enemy lines to tap their wires, a jeep, a telephone, K-rations for myself and three others, and eight pigeons.

YD's mission on the second problem, which began late Sunday afternoon, was to defend against an attack by the Blues. Kaz called his platoon leaders together at the base of a hill that evening and told us to check it out. I moved upward through my sector and at the top scouted around in the dark. Coming down I heard the sound of running feet and saw what looked like dozens of gleaming eyes. It took me several seconds to realize that a flock of sheep — as scared as I, no doubt — was scampering by.

We dug foxholes on the hillside. After posting guards, I curled up by mine and despite having no blankets or tent immediately fell asleep. 45 minutes later our First Sergeant awakened me. Breakfast, he proclaimed, "is not being served in bed, so get your goddam platoon over to the kitchen trucks." First Sergeants have a way with words, and are not impressed by the gold bars we work so hard for in OCS.

Most of the next day, according to my weekend letter home, was spent

> *pulling back and making defensive preparations. By 9 that night I was ready for some shut-eye but a runner summoned me to the battalion CP. I sat there two hours waiting for instructions from higher headquarters regarding a wire-tapping mission. Around midnight word came that the division was withdrawing, so I returned to Company E and began another march to the rear — 14 miles this time. We dug in and at noon were attacked. Rain started falling, drenching everyone. About 4 o'clock Kaz ordered my platoon to keep fighting while the battalion withdrew, then try to get away. We held off the enemy force for an hour, then were overrun. Umpires declared many of my men killed or wounded and the rest of us prisoners. I was taken to the attacking division's command post for interrogation. When I entered the intelligence officer's tent, there was Major O'Neal, captured during the withdrawal. Nobody paid any attention to me, so I stood quietly in a corner, glad to be where it was warm. After the G-2 (a Colonel) finished questioning O'Neal, he said, "Would you like to stick around and dry off?" O'Neal replied yes, so I did too. Both of them were surprised that I hadn't left; but they didn't tell me to go so I stayed. The three of us drank coffee together and listened to the Red Skelton show on his radio.*
>
> *A truck full of captured YD's picked me up. We rode the rest*

of the night, and at dawn were back where we started, the driver having lost his way. He tried again and reached the P.O.W. camp about noon. The problem ended 10 minutes later. When I rejoined Company E that evening fires were burning brightly and dinner was being prepared.

Mother, at my request, had mailed me half a pint of bourbon. Saturday afternoon, sitting cross-legged in my pup tent while a gale howled outside, I poured an ounce or so into my canteen cup, added water and some lemon powder from a C ration, heated it over a candle, and in blissful solitude sipped what at that moment seemed like the most delectable drink in the entire world.

Dad had asked what I wore during these problems, what equipment I carried, whether I walked or rode, and what we ate:

I wear long underwear, olive drab wool pants and shirt, coveralls, a field jacket, sometimes an overcoat or raincoat, gloves, two pairs of sox, leggings, G I shoes, galoshes, and a helmet liner with a steel helmet on it. My equipment consists of a carbine, a webbed belt to which my first aid packet, pouch for carbine ammunition and canteen are attached, a musette bag on my back, binoculars and gas mask container around my neck. In the musette bag are mess gear, emergency K ration, a map, extra sox, toilet articles, flashlight, candy. In my shirt pocket I have paper and pencil for writing messages, matches, and usually a pack of cigarettes even though I rarely smoke them. When engaged in combat I leave my musette bag and galoshes behind (also the overcoat, if it's not too cold) and they are picked up by trucks. My bedroll consists of two blankets and a pup tent, and is carried on our kitchen trucks, which also transport the enlisted men's barracks bags and officers' footlockers. I walk when the platoon does unless I'm on a special assignment.

In bivouac the food is good, and also ample. On the problems we have a hot breakfast before daylight if we're near the kitchen truck, and are given two sandwiches and an apple in a paper sack for lunch. For dinner the kitchen crew serves a hot meal, but often (so it seems) they can't reach us and we get nothing. The emergency K ration isn't supposed to be used unless you have gone 18 hours with no food.

Seeing Kaz move ahead without waiting for orders from higher ranking officers helped me become more aggressive. Once, he took over a nearby unit whose commander wasn't there and drove the enemy from a hill. Another time, going down a road with our company, he noticed a battery of hostile artillery guns moving through a draw and promptly assembled a group to capture them. He was excited and led the attack himself. As my self-confidence improved, so did my initiative and enthusiasm. On one of the few occasions when First Platoon was behind the company instead of out in front, I spotted an enemy force approaching the battalion flank and deployed my squads to intercept it. However, much of what we were required to do seemed purposeless or unrealistic; it was hard to be enthusiastic in those situations.

Bad weather continued to plague us. If it didn't rain it snowed, and we were cold a great deal of the time. We marched seven miles Monday with me leading the company. My instructions from Kaz, who had gone forward to reconnoiter, were to follow a narrow road. It ended abruptly in the middle of nowhere. I was wondering what to do when he appeared. That night, in an attempt to get warm, I wrapped my arms around a kettle the kitchen crew was using to heat something and sat for 15 minutes hugging it. We quit using mess kits because they filled up so quickly with rain, and instead held two slices of bread and let the mess sergeant pile our food on top of them. One morning, when the company moved out in a hurry, he dumped scrambled eggs into our bare hands so we could eat on the run. When the third problem ended we were waist-high in water, wading across a river.

Kaz gave me a 24-hour pass. A 3rd Battalion lieutenant also received one. He and I left Saturday noon for Nashville in the back of a truck loaded with enlisted men. It dropped us off downtown. We bought a pint of rum (the only thing the liquor store had), took it to a club for officers in the Hermitage Hotel, ordered set-ups, drank until the bottle was empty, ate dinner in the hotel dining room, got a haircut, shampoo, shave and some kind of facial treatment in a barber shop down the street, then went to a private home where the USO had arranged for us to spend the night. I lay in the bathtub for 30 minutes, submerged in hot water, and slept in a bed with two sheets, two blankets, a pillow and a comforter. The next morning we rode on the train to a town three miles from our bivouac area and in an army vehicle the rest of the way, arriving six minutes before our passes expired. I felt like a million dollars. This was the high point of maneuvers for me.

On the fourth problem,

> *we marched 46 miles in two days, in driving rain, through ankle-deep mud, with hardly any food and only a few hours sleep. Our feet, rubbed by soaking wet sox, were blistered and calloused. Morale couldn't have been lower. We lost 60% of our men. Of the five officers with the company (Sikorski wasn't there due to a temporary assignment at regimental headquarters) three dropped out — only Lt. Kaznolwicz and I kept on. He told me afterwards what a good job I'd done and that he will recommend me for First Lieutenant as soon as I'm eligible.*
>
> *We started out again last Monday — problem #5 this time. Again it was rain and mud and endless marching, and again I was acting Executive Officer. By Tuesday many had fallen by the wayside, unable to go any farther. As Co. E's exec, I was at the head of the battalion's advance elements. About 5 in the afternoon a messenger came up to me and said Kaz had keeled over from exhaustion. We had 30 men and one other officer left. That put me in command of the company. . . .*

We were ordered to move to a nearby hill and defend ourselves against an attack by enemy troops. I made a quick reconnaissance, assembled the surviving officer and our key noncoms, summarized my plan of defense and, unsure about what I was doing, asked for suggestions. Nobody spoke; maybe they too were unsure. I had Sgt. Hinsley set up an anti-tank outpost and the rest dig foxholes, then let those who weren't on guard duty go inside a deserted farmhouse to get warm. Theoretically, a single mortar or artillery shell could kill all of them, but this was pretend warfare and they deserved a break.

So did I, but word came that Captain Bahr wanted to see me. I had trouble finding his command post in the dark and fell once, then walked into an unseen tree branch that scratched my face and poked one eye. It was nothing serious but I let out a burst of profanity that would have shocked a drill sergeant. All of us knew plenty of dirty words and we used them freely, although not against each other. I never swore at my men, and rarely took the name of the Lord in vain. This time, however, I did: "For Christ sake, how long do I have to put up with this God damn crap?" I was cold and weary and had blisters on my feet and wondered why some stupid general thought this was good for us. Almost immediately my anger turned to remorse. "Forgive me, Lord," I whispered, plodding on, and prayed for strength to keep going.

Bahr said he needed E Company soldiers to guard the battalion CP. I replied that because of our depleted ranks we couldn't spare any. He mumbled a half-hearted warning to stay alert and dispatched his runner to find somebody else.

At daybreak O'Neal and I led what remained of the battalion toward the Cumberland River, some eight miles away. It was the division objective, which no doubt is the sole reason any of us managed to keep going. We were nearly there when the problem ended.

"Life for me these past two weeks has indeed been hard," my letter to the folks confessed:

> *I actually fell asleep while marching, which supposedly is impossible. It probably didn't last more than a few seconds but sure gave me a funny feeling when my eyes opened. I couldn't write to you last weekend because incessant rains had swollen the Tennessee streams and our company was isolated. We huddled around fires until Saturday evening when huge trucks from Quartermaster Corps hauled us out. We had to spend Sunday cleaning our rifles and equipment.*
>
> *Things are better now. Battalion headquarters is allowing us to buy beer; E Company will receive 15 cases this afternoon for 110 or so officers and enlisted men. I got a lift into Lebanon last night for a shower. Your cookies were a big hit with the platoon, Mom; we all thank you.*

Dad, en route home from visiting Mike at West Point after a business trip to New York City, wrote me a letter I saved:

> *Mike is proud of what you are doing and wishes he could serve under you. Coming from a West Pointer, that's a real tribute. It would be such a happy renunion if you could get to Lincoln in June during his leave. . . .*

You boys are my pride and joy. I miss you so much. My main interest in life is your happiness, success and welfare. I think of you all the time. . . . The longer your overseas duty is delayed, the better it is from my standpoint. I know you will do well in whatever job you're assigned.

Mom had written me that his law practice was wearing him out. For as long as I could remember, he had put in long hours, often working until late at night to support his wife and three sons and, during the 1930's, his invalid father. Now, with the two oldest boys gone, Grandfather dead, and David earning his own spending money (as Mike and I had done), Dad's income exceeded his expenses. What he wanted, and badly needed, was additional help; but almost all young lawyers were in the armed forces, and those of any age who remained were swamped. How many months or years will pass, I wondered, before I'm allowed to return, obtain my law degree and become an attorney with him?

The sixth problem began on Monday – in a downpour, of course. That night the rain turned to snow and it continued the next day. Our battalion, with Kaz in command, captured a hill. My platoon ambushed some enemy jeeps driving along a road; elated, we pressed forward and were ambushed ourselves. An umpire declared all of us casualties (wounded, captured or killed) and told me to have the platoon remain in a nearby field. The men, spotting a small country store, proceeded to buy soft drinks and snacks. This violated the rules, since the problem wasn't over, but I didn't try to stop them. Suddenly, a captain from the Inspector General's department appeared, asked questions, and made notes. The next day I had to report to General Paul. He listened to my explanation, emphasized the need for discipline, explained the key role junior officers play, fined me $25 for disobeying orders, and as I turned to leave said: "We're counting on you, Lieutenant. Don't let us down." Kaz thought it was unfair to impose a fine and claimed I "got gypped."

The seventh problem lasted until noon Friday and because of pleasant weather, "wasn't too bad." For the eighth one, O'Neal appointed me battalion liaison officer and furnished a jeep, which meant I could take my bedroll, be amply supplied with C rations, and ride instead of walk.

Sixteen privates from an Army Student Training Program unit (ASTP) were assigned to my platoon, bringing it to full strength – 40 men. "They are terrible soldiers," I wrote the folks, but that probably wasn't a fair evaluation. "Inexperienced" would have been more correct. In December, I too had been inexperienced. Now I was able to keep going with little or no sleep, insufficient food, and a minimum of drinking water; to endure cold weather in wet clothes that never dried out; to persevere despite pain, fatigue and frustration. Best of all, confidence in my ability to make sound decisions and be a leader had developed.

"What a relief to have maneuvers over," my final letter from Tennessee stated. "Those two months involved the worst suffering, in a physical sense, I've ever been through – really awful." Unfortunately, even worse suffering was yet to come.

Fortunately, I didn't know that.

4

At Fort Jackson, South Carolina, where the division went next, officers were quartered in huts. The one Dorgan, Gray, Albertson and I shared had four cots in it, plus a table and chair. A PX, a movie theater, and an Officers Club with an outdoor swimming pool were close by. Columbia, some seven miles away, was accessible by bus.

The second week after our arrival was spent in a bivouac area adjacent to the rifle range. We got up at 4:45 each morning and fired until 7:30 at night in order to improve our accuracy with the M-1 and other weapons. The following week I attended, at division headquarters, a six-day seminar on poison gas.

Near the end of April everybody received a furlough. Mine, with travel time, totaled 13 days. I rode part way in a coach but had a berth for the overnight trip from Chicago to Lincoln and enjoyed the luxury of dinner in the diner. Mom, who had learned how to mix Whiskey Sours in a cocktail shaker, managed to acquire the necessary ingredients -- lemons, sugar and bourbon -- even though they were in short supply. It felt good to be home, to see my civilian clothes hanging in the closet, to play cards with the folks and David. The war didn't appear to be limiting what he and other high school kids were able to do, at least not to any substantial degree. Things seemed much the same at the university, too, when I visited a couple of sorority houses, except that most of my friends were gone.

Gray was alone in our hut, drinking gin, when I returned to Jackson. "Help yourself," he said, pointing to the half-empty bottle. I poured a couple of ounces into my tin cup, added water from a pitcher the mess sergeant had let him borrow, took off my shoes, and relaxed. We talked for over an hour. "I married after finishing high school," he told me, "and worked in my father-in-law's hardware store until 1942, then, to avoid being drafted, volunteered and eventually got into OCS." Dorgan, he believed, was commissioned through ROTC without attending OCS and taught school until called to active duty. He didn't know how Kaz, Jud and Albertson earned their commissions. My tribulations at Benning amazed him: "God Almighty, they really put it to you! It was easy when I went through."

"Lt. Kaznolwicz says First Platoon will be the battalion's Ranger Platoon," I wrote the folks that weekend. "I'm not sure what this involves except that I have to train three-man groups in swimming, scouting and demolitions. So it's back to the grind in earnest. Luckily, the weather is perfect."

Although we worked hard during the day, spent several evenings a week in class, and continued to have field exercises, my four and a half months at Fort Jackson were pleasant ones. Each platoon leader was off duty from Saturday noon until Sunday night every other week. I swam, read *Time* magazine, attended church at a nearby chapel, drank beer or whiskey (moderately) at the Officers Club with Kaz, Jud, Dorgan, Gray, Albertson or lieutenants from other companies, and occasionally went with some of them to Columbia. On "duty" weekends, unless given battalion or regimental assignments, we could relax in our huts or go to the club if the First Sergeant knew where to find us in case problems arose.

The army created two new awards: Combat Infantryman for soldiers who performed satisfactorily on the battlefield, and Expert Infantryman for those not in combat who proved their proficiency in other ways. O'Neal scheduled a three-day bivouac to help 2nd Battalion's officers and enlisted men qualify for the Expert award. I was in charge of rifle grenade firing, and though not required to, personally took all of the tests being offered. One of them was a 25-mile forced march. Halfway through it, pain developed in both my knees. At the next ten-minute break I lay down, and when the break ended could hardly get up. The remainder of the march was pure torture but I made it to the destination, as did 90 of the 150 who started.

The following morning I put O'Neal "through his paces" on the rifle grenade range. "They're not thrown, like hand grenades," a letter to David explained, "but are shot from rifles using special cartridges and an attachment called a launcher." At officers' school Friday evening General Paul talked to us about managing men. Saturday afternoon I went with four other lieutenants to a state park ten miles away where we "soaked up sunshine and flirted with the girls."

My turn to act as Regimental Duty Officer from 5 p.m. until eight the next morning came on June 5th. You weren't allowed to sleep and had to stay close to headquarters or the guardhouse. I drove back and forth between them every so often, in a jeep, but most of the time sat at the adjutant's desk reading or dozing. Learning, when I arrrived at the guardhouse about 4 a.m., that Allied forces had begun landing in France, I joined the group crowded around a radio, excited by the realization that our troops were assaulting Hitler's *Festung Europa*, apprehensive for those participating in this historic event, and very thankful not to be one of them.

That weekend Company E had a party. Those whose wives were in Columbia brought them; the rest

> *escorted such fair flowers as they were able to pick up, or came alone. After a buffet supper that included six kegs of beer, a local group provided music. The guys in my platoon had fun bringing their partners over for me to dance with. I was kept busy (and exhausted) doing the jives these gals knew.*

The following evening one of our privates stopped me as I left the orderly room. "Thanks for dancing with my wife, Lt. Stevens," he said, "that party was the first real fun she's had since we got here. It takes all of my pay and most of what she earns waiting tables in Columbia to rent our little one-room apartment and buy groceries." My response must have encouraged him because he kept on talking: "She's awfully lonely and worries a lot about me.

We don't have children but are going to after the war. I hope this is all over with soon." I hoped so, too, and tried to be both sympathetic and encouraging, but felt that my remarks were pretty shallow.

On June 15th, Infantry Day,

> *we stood for hours in the sun while generals tossed verbal bouquets at us and tried to convince the gullible that they were certainly lucky to be in the infantry. Our under-the-breath retorts don't bear repeating. The parade was no doubt a tremendous success, but all I saw were the sweat-soaked backs of the guys ahead of me. We had the afternoon free and spent it in the pool at the Officers Club.*

Despite those caustic comments, I was impressed. Hearing YD's band play, "We are kings of the highway, the backbone of an army moving out," while thousands of soldiers in companies, battalions and regiments marched by the reviewing stand, engendered a feeling of patriotism and pride.

Friday evening we went nine miles in two hours with full field equipment, this being a requirement for the Expert Infantryman award. I made it but stated in a letter home: "What a hell of a life! I don't have trouble until after the 7th or 8th mile, then get knee pains that last about a day."

My application for transfer to the Air Corps was turned down. Mother suggested seeking a desk job. "Use your brains instead of your feet," she urged. "Higher command," I replied, "is telling college graduates their feet are what is needed most, or words to that effect. Jobs in personnel, supply, administration and the like are filled; combat slots are not. Anyway, Mom, they seem to depend on me here, so maybe I'd better stick it out. The medics will provide arch supports if my knees continue to cause trouble."

Dad, too, wished I would ask for reassignment. An orthopedic surgeon he knew was willing to submit an affidavit that more marching could result in permanent disability. I understood his concern but said no. Leaving Company E and my platoon now would be wrong. A bond had formed. We would stay together. The point of no return had been passed.

A letter the following weekend reported completing "all but the final test for Expert Infantryman. I'll catch that one next time it's offered. In the 87th Division, which is stationed at Jackson, only 600 earned it (out of almost 11,000 who were eligible)."

> *Yesterday a bunch of us went to a movie and then to Capt. Kaznolwicz's hut with a case of beer. We discussed a variety of subjects, among them West Point. When somebody mentioned that my brother is a cadet there, Kaz said to me, "If he turns out to be half as good an officer as you are, they can be proud of him." Those little shots in the arm sure do help.*
>
> *The battalion surgeon checked my knees and arches and thinks they're okay. He shaved the hair off both legs, taped my feet, and wants me to see how they hold up on our air-ground problem, which lasts 36 hours.*

It started Friday morning. We walked a lot, had no opportunity to sleep, and didn't get back until 6 p.m. Saturday. The knee pains returned but I was able to keep going and served as Battalion Duty Officer on Sunday.

In the weeks that followed I supervised BAR firing, marched in a parade for some visiting Congressmen, attended officers school, and put 64 people, including myself, through the course in pistol marksmanship. "Most of us couldn't hit the broad side of a barn but it was good experience and also fun." The company practiced disarming mines and booby traps and participated in an attack behind advancing tanks – "we, of course, being on foot." One Saturday afternoon I helped supervise a three-hour session of "organized athletics," which consisted of playing games in a lake. That night Gray, Dorgan and I bought a bottle of bourbon in Columbia and got "pleasantly lit."

Kaz was promoted to Captain. O'Neal became a Lieutenant Colonel. No shavetails were promoted, he explained, because the division's quota of first lieutenants was filled.

One of our field problems involved fighting in a village. We shot at cardboard targets that simulated enemy riflemen hiding in doorways, leaning against window sills, and kneeling on rooftops. Real soldiers, concealed and well-protected, fired live ammunition over our heads. After my platoon finished, the battalion S-3 had me go with another group to "critiquc" its performance. Something went wrong and a man was killed. "I accompanied the squad on the right side of the street," my "Disclosure Of Facts" stated:

> *Pvt. Chase's squad was on the opposite side. I walked behind the squad leader. A staff sergeant carrying a red flag was ahead of him. When we were about one-third of the way into the village I heard shouts of "cease firing" and ordered everybody to lock their rifles. It was impossible for me to tell who fired the shot that hit Pvt. Chase, when it was fired, or where it was fired from.*
>
> *At the orientation before the problem began, Lt. Ambrose informed all participants that they were to fire at silhouette targets on the opposite side of the street and to fire only in front of the soldier with the red flag. He repeated this several times and it seemed to be clearly understood by everyone.*
>
> *William D. Stevens*
> *2d Lt., 101st Inf.*

Once in awhile I wished the war would end so I could return to Lincoln and get on with my life, but those occasions were rare. Our troops in Europe and the Far East were having a tough time; clearly, much fighting lay ahead — a lot remained to be done. When sirens awakened me one night, I wondered whether they meant an armistice had been declared and thought how fantastic this would be. The smell of smoke terminated that reverie; our theater was on fire.

My platoon went to a remote part of Fort Jackson for a three-day self-sustaining patrol through hostile territory. We were to follow a pre-arranged route 55 miles long, obtain drinking water from streams, steal food from the enemy if our K rations ran out, and use pigeons (furnished by division headquarters) to send back messages. Nobody accompanied us — no umpires, observers or other officers. We had to keep moving — 55 miles was a lot to cover in 72 hours — but did manage to sleep a little. No enemy rations were found and we failed to locate drinkable water. I had minimal knee pains but got poison oak on my face and both hands. In spite of these and other difficulties, we accomplished the mission. My report to O'Neal said:

> *The leader of an enemy patrol was taken prisoner by our First*

> *Squad. He revealed that their instructions were to capture someone from this squad but the alertness of our sentries prevented them from doing so. . . .*
>
> *Denying soldiers sufficient water causes unnecessary impairment of health, efficiency and morale. . . .*
>
> *A man is not a machine; he must have rest – not just enough rest to keep him functioning physically and not just enough to keep up his morale, but enough to keep his mind and senses keen and alert. The army recognizes this in "Psychology For The Fighting Man," Field Manual 21-75 . . .*
>
> *Why are patrols in hostile territory required to shave? Several of my NCO's complained about this and I couldn't come up with a satisfactory answer.*

It was now clear that I had what it took to lead the platoon. Mahlin and Mulvaney did also, but neither of them tried to second-guess or embarrass me. My biggest concern was how strict to be. "When to ease up and when to bear down is a constant problem," I commented in a note to the folks. Letting rain-soaked guys who weren't on guard duty dry off in an empty farmhouse during maneuvers struck me as okay; not disciplining those who broke the rules by buying stuff at a store had been wrong. "Be tough, Lieutenant; make 'em squirm," Mulvaney urged at the start of a platoon inspection. I tried to be strict but tended toward leniency.

Each of my three squads consisted of a sergeant, a corporal, and ten privates or privates first class, all except one armed with M-1 rifles; the other had a BAR. In addition to these 36, the platoon included Mahlin, Mulvaney, a sniper, and a runner who carried messages to the company CP and, if I was busy, dug my foxhole. I knew everybody in the platoon and, to some extent, their strengths and limitations. A few weren't very smart but none of them appeared to be stupid and none seemed uncooperative. Whether any had personal problems was impossible for me to judge since officers stayed out of the enlisted men's barracks unless they had a valid reason to go in. Did the non-coms who lived there do more than provide supervision; did they help those who needed help, encourage those who needed encouragement? Would a non-com be aware of it if someone had a problem, or realize that a problem might be developing? Mahlin assured me that everything was all right.

Is there anybody in the platoon who should be weeded out, I wondered – anybody who's not dependable enough or sufficiently well-trained to face enemy soldiers in combat? I didn't think so. Those that joined us near the end of maneuvers were ready, according to their squad leaders, who had exerted extra effort to bring them along and, during our field problems, paired them with experienced soldiers. Most of the men who'd been in the division since 1941, tired of make-believe warfare, were anxious to go overseas; "Let's use what we've learned and get the job done," one of them told me. Even I, a part of YD for only seven months, was becoming restless.

"Mail censorship may begin soon so omit whatever you don't want the government to read," a July 17th letter warned the family. We'd been notified that the division would leave for a Port of Embarkation in mid-August.

I've been handling legal and quasi-legal matters in our company ever since we arrived at Jackson. They include acting as War Bond officer, insurance officer, voting officer (to help those who want to vote in November), personal affairs officer, etc. Today I was appointed assistant regimental claims officer, with the job of investigating accidents and incidents involving injury to persons or property. That may entail additional work but it could be good training. Captain Kaznolwicz and I received the Expert Infantryman award, as did quite a few of our non-coms and privates. Notwithstanding all of this, life here is pretty enjoyable: a bed to sleep in, latrines with hot and cold running water, three meals a day, and at least a couple of nights each week for relaxation. I still remember maneuvers, so these things mean a lot. Yesterday Lt. Albertson and his wife invited me to dinner in Columbia. They rent a tiny apartment from a hospitable woman there.

Dad, I signed a Will naming you my executor. The enclosed sheet lists your rights if I am killed, or so badly wounded that I can't contact you, or missing or captured or interned in a neutral country. If I don't make it, give Mike my fishing tackle and David my portable typewriter. You get my war bonds and whatever is in my bank account – pretty meager repayment for all you've done for me but I guess dads don't expect repayment, do they?

On Monday the division went out for a three-day problem in defense. That night I crept forward alone to study the terrain enemy troops would come across to attack us. Stars filled the sky. I stared at them in wonder and recalled the evening Mike and I slept in our backyard so we could watch for meteors. The darkness didn't bother me then because there were two of us. Now, alone on a South Carolina hillside, uneasiness returned.

This time it was justified, for 50 yards off to my left, moving silently toward a wooded area, I spied a line of advancing soldiers silhouetted against the starlit horizon. Stepping into the trees behind me to avoid being seen by them, I came face to face with a man and, startled, reached for my trench knife. "It's okay, Lieutenant," a voice whispered; "being out here is dangerous, so I followed you." It was Mulvaney. We hurried to where our sentries were posted, alerted them and the rest of the platoon, sent my runner to tell Kaz, and had a squad sergeant lead a patrol through the woods to locate the approaching column. They returned 30 minutes later, unable to find it. Mulvaney and I tried; we too were unsuccessful. Chagrined, I doubled the number of sentries, told everyone else to go back to sleep, and spent the remainder of the night by my foxhole peering wide-eyed into the darkness.

Saturday evening five or six of us got into a discussion at the Officers Club about "what we're fighting for." For democracy, somebody suggested, "the right to a voice in how you're governed." Frank Beattie, an H Company lieutenant I liked, disagreed. "We're fighting for freedom from regimentation," he argued; "freedom isn't free, you have to work for it, risk your life for it." Others believed this was "too ethereal." "We're fighting Japan because they bombed our ships," one of them asserted, "and Germany because they declared war against us." Carter, the battalion S-4, thought 90% of our enlisted men hadn't any idea what they're fighting for. "How about the remaining 10%; do they?" I asked. "Probably not," he replied, "maybe none of us know." Dorgan pointed out that everybody in the regiment had seen the film, *Why We Fight*; what did it say? None of us could remember. We talked for quite awhile. The consensus seemed to be that the war was being fought to keep Germany, Japan and other aggressors from taking what they want. That's why America assisted England prior to the attack at Pearl Harbor. We're fighting to preserve each country's right to its own land, its own way of life.

Later, thinking about this, I wondered if my willingness to go overseas with the 26th Division represented an altruistic impulse to fight for freedom. No, not really, I decided. Was it the result of patriotic eagerness to help my country by meeting the enemy in combat? Definitely not; getting shot at didn't appeal to me at all; why risk being killed. My desire for overseas service, I concluded, sprang from egotism. I was thrilled, as a little boy, when Dad told me about his exploits in the Balloon Corps during World War One, and disappointed when I learned he hadn't left the United States. Landing on foreign soil would keep my children and friends from feeling this way about me. It might not even be necessary to fight: what scenario could be more perfect than for YD to reach the front the day the war ended!

On August 5th, Kaz offered me a four-day pass to visit Mike at West Point. My parents decided to join us and make it a spur-of-the-moment family reunion. Our plans almost fell apart: Kaz discovered that passes for officers had to be issued by Regimental Headquarters and couldn't exceed 72 hours. Colonel Scott, the 101st's C. O., came to the rescue by granting me emergency leave from Friday morning to Monday night and directing the Post Transportation Office to arrange plane and train reservations.

Mother, Dad and David were waiting when I landed at LaGuardia. We toasted each other with Whiskey Sours at the Waldorf, saw the new musical *Oklahoma*, had dinner on the Starlight Roof, and the next morning rode a bus to Newburgh. The snappy salutes I got from Mike and his room mates, and from other cadets as we walked around, made me feel more like the Commander-in-Chief than a 2nd lieutenant. We ate with him Sunday noon, at a restaurant, joking and laughing as if none of us had a care in the world, then returned to Manhattan (without Mike), watched a major league baseball game, and went to Billy Rose's Diamond Horseshoe. Monday, at the railway station, on a concrete platform by my coach, the folks and I said goodbye. It was a difficult moment for them: tears flowed from Mother's eyes and there may have been some in Dad's – he turned away once to brush a finger across his cheek. I hugged him, kissed Mom, climbed aboard, waved through a window, and realized as the train began moving that this may have been our last time together.

The company started packing the next day. Gray asked if he could buy my alarm clock; his wife needed one and they were hard to obtain. I hesitated since not sending it home might indicate that I wouldn't be coming back, an attitude no soldier should have, then said okay and removed it from the box in which I was mailing my undershirts and shorts to Lincoln "because they're white and we have to wear olive drab ones overseas."

"By now most of the division has gone," my final letter from Ft. Jackson reported. "Don't worry about me. Others appear to have done the dirtiest fighting and probably old YD will never see combat anyway. All is well."

Those lines, written to reassure them, didn't express my true feelings. I believed old YD would see combat, probably in Europe after a brief stop in England. It might be true that the dirtiest fighting was over; Allied units occupied part of northern France and had started advancing south and east; surely Germany would not be able to hold out much longer, nor want to. On the other hand, her leaders were fanatics and they commanded well-trained armies. Even a mop-up operation could be dangerous. If our destination was the Far East, going from island to island might take months. Having received no instruction in jungle warfare, it seemed unlikely that we would be sent to the Pacific, but logic didn't always prevail in the armed forces.

On August 19th, in the haze of early dawn, Company E assembled on the parade ground with the rest of 2nd Battalion. Everyone had a duffle bag in addition to his weapon and his back pack or musette bag. "Did Helen like the alarm clock?" I asked Gray as we stood waiting. "I don't know," he answered; "she spent the weekend in tears begging me not to leave. I tried to explain to her that there's no turning back now."

Dorgan overheard us. His wife was in Columbia also. "That's right," he said with sadness in his voice, "there's no turning back now. And for some, probably, there'll be no coming back."

Platoons were forming; I saw Mahlin organizing ours. The dim light made everything seem unreal. I felt like a spectator watching a strange, ghostly drama. It was hard to realize that the division would soon be doing what it had prepared for so thoroughly. Dorgan's remark – "For some, probably, there'll be no coming back" – lingered in my mind.

One by one our companies marched to and boarded a troop train. The battalion's lieutenants rode together in a Pullman car. We piled our gear in the ladies' restroom, then located the seats assigned to us. Before long the train began moving and Fort Jackson faded out of sight.

A kitchen crew came down the aisle with breakfast: scrambled eggs, bacon, bread and butter, an orange and coffee. Decks of cards appeared; Poker, Pitch, Black Jack and Gin Rummy games began. I played awhile, read, dozed, and gazed at the passing countryside. The battalion S-3 announced that we were en route to Camp Shanks, New York. In mid-afternoon, KP's brought another meal. At 10 p.m. each platoon leader checked on his men. Most of mine were in army sleeping car bunks. I chatted with several, signed the duty roster to show I'd been around, headed back, and in my berth, listening to the wheels clickety clack as they raced along the rails, wondered what Fate had in store for General Paul's 26th Division – and for me.

At Camp Shanks we learned how to censor letters and were issued impregnated clothing for use in event of a chemical attack. A few days later I went with the regiment's advance party to New Jersey, and by boat from there to Manhattan's "Pier 42, U. S. Army Port of Embarkation." A captain called out names; when he reached Stevens, I joined the line ascending an enclosed flight of narrow stairs. The duffle bag on my shoulder bumped from one wall to the other as I staggered up the steps; my binoculars case and gas mask container swung back and forth wildly; the butt of my carbine banged noisily against a metal railing. At the top, one corner of the sack holding my bag lunch gave way and a hard-boiled egg flew to the concrete floor, where it disintegrated into a thousand pieces. The lieutenant beside me, grinning, said, "I hope that's not an omen of how things will be overseas." I hoped so too. At the gangplank somebody handed me a slip marked V3. "Your room number," he mumbled.

Our ship, the *Saturnia*, had been an Italian luxury liner. V3 was the bridal suite, which I would share with 15 or 16 other lieutenants. Metal bunks rose three-high along the walls. Gene Tunney and his bride, we were told, occupied this cabin – minus the extra beds, presumably – on their honeymoon. After dumping my stuff, I stood on the deck with Frank Beattie looking at New York City. A ferry boat loaded with passengers crept by. "Are they proud of us, knowing we're soldiers about to go overseas?" he asked; "Grateful for what we're doing?" My answer was, "Neither, perhaps; maybe they don't care."

When the regiment arrived, I led E Company to its area, helped them get settled, and remained there until Albertson relieved me.

The next day the *Saturnia* and other transports moved slowly into the Atlantic, where navy craft of various shapes and sizes took places around them. Our "armada," according to a YD history published later, consisted of 101 vessels "of all classes": aircraft carriers, luxury liners, destroyers, cruisers "and humble victory ships." It was an impressive sight. We appeared to be going north-east, toward Europe, I assumed. Where in Europe? England? France? The Mediterranean?

Officers ate in the main dining salon, at tables with linen napkins and tablecloths. Its mirrors and murals had been boarded over; even so, the room was fantastic. So were our meals, one in the morning and one in the afternoon, served by Italian waiters in white jackets. What a way to travel!

On our third night at sea I was Regimental Duty Officer. About 4 a.m., standing alone in an unenclosed area near the stern, I recalled the happiness of my growing up years and pondered why a peace-loving person like me should be crossing the ocean to wage war against another nation. I felt no affection for the Germans – the aggression of their *Führer* had caused all this – but didn't hate them either. Was I supposed to?

Listening to unseen waves lap at our ship as it moved silently through the darkness, I hoped for a safe return, partly because so much of what I'd done before my military service began was in preparation for the future, partly because I knew my death would be such a devastating blow to Mother and Dad; then, for the first time, gave serious thought to the fact that I might be badly wounded or killed. Would a bullet ripping into my body cause intense pain? Would I cry out or remain silent? Realize that death was approaching? If my life ended, would I then be with God? Is He aware of me on this ocean liner far from home, I wondered. Will He help me meet whatever challenges come my way? Will I measure up to those challenges, or be fearful and falter? Do I have sufficient courage to lead the platoon against experienced Nazi troops? Will I know what to do, when called upon to face them, and be able to do it? My greatest concern, as I contemplated what lay ahead, was not death but failure.

Time passed slowly. We had 15 minutes of calesthenics each day. Books, magazines, movies and a mini-PX were available. Somebody played an ocarina; another sang; clusters of enlisted men shot Craps. Once in awhile, leaning on a railing, I surveyed the vast expanse of water that stretched in every direction as far as the eye could see, and at the ships surrounding us. Could a submarine slip by them? It seemed unlikely; still, U-Boat commanders were clever and had struck many a convoy. I wasn't worried; but knowing our foe might be out there, waiting for an opportunity to destroy us, brought home the reality of war.

Occasionally planes flew over; and, twice, blimps headed in the opposite direction. I read *The Apostle*, *The Razor's Edge*, *My Son, My Son* and several mystery stories; saw what appeared to be a whale; and one afternoon, although it was off-limits, strolled nonchalantly into navy officers "country," where a friendly ensign showed me around. Now and then the sea was rough and people got sick. My 24th birthday passed unnoticed because I purposely kept quiet about it.

Censoring letters the men of First Platoon wrote made me feel like an intruder peeking into their private lives. I tried to skip the personal parts but, without intending to, found myself reading the tender sentiments some of them contained. Many reflected the writer's deep religious faith. None revealed fear, though one said, "I know I will never see you again."

When we emerged from the bridal suite on September 7th,

land was not more than a mile or two away and our ship had dropped anchor. O'Neal called us together and gave instructions for disembarking. "The city you are looking at," he stated, "is Cherbourg, on the coast of France."

I scrutinized it with my field glasses. The harbor was full of damaged vessels, a few upright, some upside down, others listing or floating on their sides. Troops were being taken ashore on huge rafts. I walked to the edge of the deck and saw a cargo net that extended to the waves below. "Good Lord," I murmured, "how am I going to get down this thing with all my equipment?" The enclosed stairway at Pier 42 had been difficult enough.

By the time our turn came, rain was falling. I put my carbine over one shoulder, my duffle bag over the other, climbed across the railing, and began my descent. The ship rocked from side to side. Our raft, riding the swells, seemed tiny and far away. My duffle bag made me top-heavy. The binoculars case and gas mask container hanging from my neck caught in the ropes of the cargo net; every so often my carbine did, too. Wouldn't it be great, I thought – sarcastically, but not without concern as the rain continued – if my hands slipped and I fell into the ocean!

No mishaps occurred. When the raft was full, it started for the shore. Ahead lay Fortress Europe.

5

The trucks that were supposed to meet us didn't show up. Kaz rushed off to find out what had gone wrong. While we waited, I studied Cherbourg. Buildings with missing walls, dangling floors, and collapsed roofs were mute evidence of war's destructiveness.

Vehicles finally arrived. The narrow country roads they traversed passed through villages where townspeople waved American flags and, when the column slowed down, handed us cups of wine or cider. We threw them cigarettes, which even little children lit and smoked.

Some of our drivers, falling behind, missed a turn and got lost. As a result my platoon reached the bivouac area after most of the battalion had finished putting up their pup tents. I pitched mine in an apple orchard assigned to E Company, visited with Mahlin about security, and wrote the folks that I was "in France." Disclosing where in France was prohibited.

The next day, to stay in shape, the platoon marched to a village that consisted of a small church, a cemetery, and 20 or 30 houses. Kids crowded around us, saying, "Gum, chum," or "Bon bon." We gave them what we had. No adults appeared, although a few looked out their windows. On an "orientation hike" the following afternoon we skirted innumerable shell holes, stared at destroyed buildings, examined a huge German gun concealed in an abandoned structure, walked past foxholes dug by soldiers who not too many weeks earlier were fighting here, avoided places marked to show they hadn't been cleared of mines, and with mixed emotions watched a convoy of trucks transporting replacements to the front.

Each morning, platoon leaders put their men through an hour of physical training and close-order drill. We also worked on marksmanship, listened to lectures about staying healthy, participated in athletic activities, and attended open-air movies. I was on our company volleyball team, umpired softball games, saw *Mrs. Miniver* for the third time, and played Poker twice in O'Neal's headquarters tent.

Occasionally we ran short of food. When that happened the cooks provided bread and peanut or apple butter for us to fill up on. "Everybody is served (and required to eat) cooked cereal for breakfast to replace the natural Vitamin G lost in dehydrating fruits and vegetables for overseas shipment," I remarked in a note to David. We received a daily issue of gum, candy and cigarettes, and once in awhile D-bars – rectangular blocks of enriched chocolate created for use as an emergency ration. Being a "chocoholic," I nibbled on one whenever possible. Apples could be picked from nearby trees but they weren't very appetizing.

One day Dorgan and I drove the company jeep to a supply depot. We went through towns that were little more than piles of rubble and saw the beaches where Allied troops landed on D-Day. They were littered with abandoned equipment, broken boxes, empty cartons, and the remains of obstacles constructed to impede our men and machines. Each of us bought a pair of combat boots and a bottle of Scotch. Liquor and good wine were difficult to obtain, but Calvados, an alcoholic beverage that in my opinion tasted like kerosene, was readily available.

Kaz told me about a young French woman who, for cigarettes or food, "had sex" with officers. She lived with her parents in a nearby village. The battalion medics, he commented, would furnish condoms and prophylactic kits for use in preventing "infection." I hesitated; for some reason going there seemed wrong. Kaz shrugged his shoulders at my less than enthusiastic response, wondering, no doubt, if I was shell-shocked already. That evening I wondered too. This was part of being overseas, something soldiers did, a perquisite of foreign service. What kept me from jumping at the opportunity? I'd had a little experience along these lines (very little) and even gone to a whorehouse once, not as a customer but with three other guys to see what the inside of one looked like. It seemed improbable, therefore, that moral values made me hesitate. Could it be idealism – a feeling that we were here to help these people and shouldn't take advantage of them? Or was it fear of "infection," or simply that being greeted at the door by her mother and father would embarrass me? I didn't know the answer – and still don't.

One evening a corporal ran toward my tent. "I think Sgt. Cherney is drunk," he said; "You'd better come over." Cherney, who obviously was feeling no pain, leered as I approached. "Get the hell out of here, Lieutenant; I don't need you," he snapped.

If he'd said it in a decent way, I might have left and let Mahlin or one of the other NCO's handle the situation. This, however, was a challenge, not a request. Our men had gathered around. I felt like demoting him to private then and there – Kaz would have backed me up – but he was too good a non-com to lose. "You're right, Sgt. Cherney," I replied, standing in front of him, "you don't need me. What you need is to have your head stuck in a pail of cold water. Someday, though, you are going to need me and I'm going to need you. Someday we're all going to need each other. When the war ends you can get as drunk as you like and I'll get drunk with you. Until then, you can't. Sober him up, Sgt. Mahlin; I want Cherney bright and shiny at reveille tomorrow, commanding his squad."

Mahlin immediately stepped forward, answered, "Yes, sir," and saluted. That impressed the members of our platoon who were standing there. We didn't salute each other except on formal occasions. Coupled with his crisp, respectful "Yes, sir," it confirmed that I was in charge and that discipline would be enforced.

On September 10th a letter from mother, written the 3rd, arrived. They hadn't heard from me since the division left Fort Jackson. "The French people," my reply reported,

> *look tattered and tired. Many towns have been damaged by bullets and shells. The fields are green in spite of war, but there are*

remnants of German equipment in most of them. I've seen all kinds of stuff lying around, including letters from home to Nazi soldiers. A Red Cross mobile unit brought us hot coffee and doughnuts – a nice treat.

We're not allowed to write specific information, so you won't know much about what I'm doing. Sorry. . . . I hope you are fine. Don't worry, all is well here.

Rumors regarding where YD would be sent began circulating. To Brest, some thought, an important seaport the allies had been unable to capture. Others believed we were going to guard army warehouses against looting. That sounded great – tolerable living conditions, little danger, and "bragging rights" for having served overseas. Nothing official appeared.

I wrote the folks every few days. "It really upsets me," one letter stated, "that workers in the United States are striking. No matter how bad things may be for those guys, they are with their families and have a roof over their heads and beds to sleep in, which is a lot more than we can say." Another mentioned that several of my men "had a meal in a French farm home – eggs, milk, bread, homemade butter, and wine. The people would accept only three francs (six cents) although the boys offered them 100."

I won't be a hero but at least I'm doing more than fight the battle of Tennessee. Nothing will make me happier than setting foot again on American soil.

A note sent shortly before our departure from Normandy said at the end: "It's peaceful and quiet here. A big full moon is shining. I'm in a rest area, far from the fronts you read about. Thanks for your reassuring words. Keep writing."

Frank Beattie and I had sat under that same moon the previous night, sipping Scotch from my bottle. Both of us planned to be attorneys. We discussed what practicing law would be like and what we hoped to accomplish. "We'll have more control over our lives then," Frank declared. "We haven't any now. Everybody gets orders telling him what to do." I nodded in agreement.

The folks and my brothers wrote regularly even though none of my letters had reached them. Mother, a U.S.O. volunteer, was helping at the railroad station when troop trains came through. One had been full of German P.O.W.'s captured after D-Day:

> *Their attitude was arrogant, superior and thoroughly detestable. An M.P. said most of them still expect to win the war. Others claim they will come back and "get us" in 25 years. . . .*
>
> *Oh, my dear, I wish I knew whether everything is all right with you. I believe the commentators are wrong in anticipating peace soon. I hope the fact that we haven't heard for so long is not a bad sign. My love, my thoughts and my prayers are with you always, wherever you may be.*

Dad feared that Germany would "fight to the bitter end" and "cause tremendous casualties before she is defeated."

> *Perhaps if we break through the Siegfried Line they will realize the hopelessness of their situation. . . .*
>
> *We think of you constantly. I awake at night and early in the morning wondering where your division has gone and what it is doing, and pray that you are safe and not too uncomfortable. A world of love from your devoted family.*

On September 25th they received my "the fields are green" letter. By then YD's fate had been determined. We were to join Patton's Third Army, battling German forces in Lorraine. My parents didn't know this, of course, and continued to write. Mother surmised that our division

> *must be at or near the front if a Red Cross mobile unit brought you coffee and doughnuts. I listen intently to the news and have placed you with the Ninth Army, which they say is in reserve for a big push.*
>
> *Oh, honey, don't do anything foolhardy. Being a German prisoner is better than being seriously wounded. Mabel Waters says she feels a sense of relief now that Tom is a P.O.W. She has heard from him twice.*

"It looks like Germany will be able to hold out until spring," a letter from dad declared:

> *This will mean a tough winter for you. I wish there were some way I could help. If I could be fighting with you or, even better, in your place, I gladly would. It is tragic that you young men who are*

in no way responsible for the war must fight it. I know you will do a good job. The nearer you come to actual combat – perhaps you are already in it – the more I realize how much you mean to me and how lucky our family was to have so many wonderful years together.

I wish you could tell us whether you have been in combat or soon will be, also which Army you are a part of and where you are now.

Both of them frequently mentioned the upcoming presidential election. They had been anti-Roosevelt since he first ran in 1932. After his victory in 1940 Dad suspected that democracy was in danger of annihilation. A fourth term would make it inevitable. The "isms" of those days – communism, fascism, socialism – were considered by Dad and most of his friends to be jeopardizing America's freedom. They thought FDR's New Deal would lead to socialism. "We will win the World War," he asserted, "but whether we can prevent the destruction of our democratic way of life is questionable."

David described what was happening in Lincoln. Mike wrote about West Point. Victories against Notre Dame and Navy would mean a perfect season for its football team. The folks, he noted, "are pretty lonely and worried."

I can't figure out where you are but imagine you're going through plenty of hell. We all miss you and pray that the Lord will watch over you. When this ends I'll be damn proud to walk down the street at your side.

Dad, concerned because there had been no word from me for more than a month, wrote on October 29th:

All we can do now is hope and pray that God will bring you through safely. If He does, the rest of my life will be filled with efforts to show my gratitude. The Lord never gave anyone a finer son, and you brought a world of happiness to me.

Goodbye, dear boy, a world of love to you.

Perhaps he felt that I had already died and was bidding me farewell. Saying "brought" instead of "have brought" and "Goodbye, dear boy," makes it sound that way.

The unbelievable destruction we passed after leaving the Normandy peninsula awed me: towns in which no structure remained intact; some, like Saint-Lo, virtually levelled; fields with gaping shell holes, uprooted hedgerows, blasted farm buildings, abandoned tanks, vehicles and guns. When the driver of the truck I was riding in got tired, I took his place for awhile and pictured my parents' amazement if they could see me behind the wheel of an army two-and-a-half-ton six-by-six loaded with infantrymen, crossing war-torn France.

We spent the night at Fontainebleau, pitching tents on the lawn of an elegant chateau, as others before us had done. The following afternoon our vehicles halted along a country road northeast of Nancy and people began jumping out of them. I hopped down from the cab of mine just as the Operations Officer came by in a jeep. He stopped, pointed to a field, yelled, "Company E will bivouac there; post guards and have everybody dig foxholes," then roared away in a cloud of dust,

Uncertain why the order was given to me rather than someone else, and seeing no sign of Kaz or Jud, I looked over the designated location, decided how to allocate it among the company's four platoons, told Dorgan, Gray, Albertson and Mahlin what we'd been instructed to do, and was about to rejoin First Platoon when Kaz showed up. He listened to my summary of developments, then left. Jud appeared a moment later. After reporting to him I went to where my men were digging in, to supervise and encourage them, but almost immediately was summoned to O'Neal's headquarters. "The U. S. 4th Armored Division is on the front line a couple of miles east of us," he told two other officers and me. "YD relieves them tomorrow. You three are being sent ahead to check out the zone assigned to 2nd Battalion."

A jeep drove us along rough, winding roads to a partially destroyed building where we examined maps of our own and enemy positions. A major described what to expect from German artillery and "screaming meemee's." I ended up by a CP that consisted of several foxholes and a half-track (an army vehicle with tank treads at the rear instead of wheels). Four enlisted men were discussing something; nearby, a lieutenant with a razor in his hand and lather on his face was peering into a small mirror. "General Patton fines anybody who isn't clean-shaven," he explained, and while showing me around mentioned more than once the importance of keeping out of sight "if you don't want your head shot off." I assured him that I didn't.

We were at the base of a hill, one of several in a line extending north and south. His company occupied its western slope. The eastern slope was unoccupied. Beyond it were the Germans.

I was given a K ration for supper and shown which foxhole to use if the need arose. "This is unreal," I said to myself after he left; "nothing's happening." I had supposed that at the front there would be officers shouting commands, soldiers charging back and forth, medics caring for the wounded, all kinds of noise and confusion, possibly even signs of terror. Instead, below the crest of the hill men were nonchalantly eating, talking, or resting. Along the summit cigarette smoke drifted from foxholes. Lying in the grass beside mine, observing all of this, I fell asleep.

The sound of a tree branch breaking awakened me. I reached for my carbine and, heart pounding, stared into the darkness. A sentry had stepped on it, I concluded, and relaxed, but sleep was slow in returning.

I wandered around alone the next morning, trying to determine how the terrain could best be utilized. It appeared that 4th Armored's arrangement wouldn't work for us because we had considerably more men.

E Company arrived about noon. Jud and the platoon leaders accepted my recommendations on how to divide the area; Kaz rushed off to see for himself. A moment later we heard artillery shells and without hesitation hit the ground. They passed over and landed half a mile away. The 4th Armored guys, who knew from its sound whether an approaching shell would come down near them, smiled and winked at each other.

Kaz came back and pointed to where he wanted each platoon. Mahlin and I started up the hill with First Squad, having instructed Second and Third Squads to wait until we signalled for them. Dorgan's platoon was on our right. Gray's, ahead of it, was near the top of the hill. I wanted to shout, "Keep out of sight," but didn't.

All of a sudden an artillery barrage began falling on our position. Each of us dove for the nearest foxhole. "Pull your butt down," the occupant of the one I went into admonished; I hastily complied. The earth trembled, shrapnel flew by my head, and dirt cascaded through the air as shell after shell exploded. I wasn't afraid, but knew that if any of them landed beside or on me the result would most likely be instantaneous death.

When they stopped, First Squad hastened to its sector and commenced digging. Dorgan walked over to where I was standing. The barrage, he said, killed a member of Gray's platoon and had seriously injured three. Shortly after that I saw Jud and, concerned about another artillery attack, suggested not bringing up my other two squads right away. He agreed and hurried on.

Half an hour later, Benson, our runner, told me First Platoon was being moved to another hill. "Why? What the hell's going on?" I exclaimed, and muttering under my breath headed for the company CP.

Kaz, seated on an ammunition box, calmly eating a C ration, described the revised plan. I cooled off, had his orderly inform Mahlin, and arranged to check out the new position with a non-com from battalion headquarters who had been to it. Benson arrived to accompany me.

We followed a circuitous route – "so the enemy won't spot us," our guide claimed – and ended up where there wasn't a sign of anyone. I assumed that we were lost, then noticed several camouflaged half-tracks and, in concealed foxholes, 4th Armored Division soldiers. A sergeant agreed to take us to his platoon leader, Lt. Crane, "in a few minutes." When I offered to find him myself, before it got dark, he advised me not to. "Stay down," somebody yelled. "Okay," I replied; but was irked because what little light remained would soon be gone and I hadn't the remotest idea where we were.

Finally the four of us started forward, only to discover, upon reaching our destination, that Crane had just left with Lt. Timmons from one of 2nd Battalion's other companies. Night had fallen but we eventually located them. I mentioned the change of plans to Timmons; he was surprised and complained that things appeared to be all fouled up. Crane thought we should talk to his C.O., Captain Voss, who had been briefed on the situation. Voss explained it to us in detail, arranged for Benson and me to go to our new area so I could look it over, and while we waited for a jeep said, "You'll do all right, Lieutenant. Don't be afraid, and always send in requisitions before you run out of something, even if it's necessary to lie."

A 4th Armored NCO drove us along make-shift roads to a country lane that had tall poplar trees on either side. We went a short distance on it, then turned and lurched cross-country toward two hills dimly outlined against the horizon. He stopped at the base of a saddle between them and walked up it with us to a platoon CP. The sergeant in charge led me through the darkness to the east face of a knoll we were to occupy. His men had foxholes there and would share them with mine until the 4th pulled out at 3 a.m. Each foxhole, he reported, was wide enough for two and deep enough to sit up in.

Our driver took Benson and me back to the road, dropped us, and sped off in the opposite direction. We made our way to where Mahlin was waiting with the platoon. I outlined what we were going to do, then, hoping not to get lost, apprehensively set out with the squads following in single file, located the tree-lined lane, turned at the proper place, spotted the two hills, and reached the saddle. Leaving Mulvaney, Benson and a private named Schieffen behind, I guided the rest to 4th Armored's foxholes and at each one whispered to two of my men: "Stay here with these guys. They leave at 0300. One of you be alert at all times. Don't fire unless you have to. I'll come back later."

Mahlin returned with me to the saddle. There, munching on a D-bar, I thought about what had taken place since noon: an artillery barrage, Company E's first casualties, a revised plan that required me to leave the position I'd spent all morning studying and go to an isolated, unfamiliar one facing concealed German troops. This was not at all what I'd expected; but unlike the previous evening, it didn't seem unreal. The war now seemed very real indeed.

At 0400, I went to where our three squads were. Somebody,

hearing me approach, called "Halt." I answered with the password. Although this wasn't the correct procedure, his challenge showed they were on the ball. I visited with those not sleeping, accepted a squad leader's suggestion that my one per foxhole on alert order be changed to two per squad, and cautioned them, before departing, to "keep down when it's light because the enemy is only a few hundred yards away." At the CP, I talked with Schieffen, who was standing guard while the others slept, then, worn out, lay on the ground and was soon dead to the world.

At daybreak, after eating a K ration for breakfast, I walked through the woods on top of the knoll to where it began sloping downward. Below me, on the exposed front of this protruding finger of land, were my men. Beyond them, fields with hedges, fences, shrubbery or stone walls on one or more sides covered the gently rolling countryside. Trees grew at the edges of some, in the middle of a few, in groves elsewhere. Here and there a ridge or hill loomed up. I saw no barns, sheds, houses or people.

Kaz, sounding like a small army, came thrashing through the underbrush behind me. We studied the area with our binoculars. An advance by YD today or tomorrow was improbable, he believed, because not all of its units were in place; for that very reason, German attacks preceded by artillery barrages should be anticipated. I hoped the barrages wouldn't start before we got back to where foxholes offered protection. There were none up here and the woods made us even more vulnerable to artillery shells that explode when they strike something solid. If the "something solid" is a tree trunk instead of the ground, those razor-sharp metal fragments hurtle down as well as sideways.

"The Krauts have combat and reconnaissance patrols out," he warned. "Tell your platoon to shoot anyone who doesn't know the password."

Combat patrols attempt to create confusion, cause casualties, take prisoners, and lower morale, then withdraw. Reconnaissance patrols seek information – "intelligence"; they avoid being seen or heard and often operate at night.

Mahlin and I felt that our CP was too far from the east slope. We found a spot on the south side of the knoll which was closer but not visible to the enemy, spent a couple of hours digging foxholes there, and when it got dark checked on the squads. It had been a tough day for them, unable to stretch out or walk around, but nobody grumbled and morale seemed to be good. "Hey, Lieutenant, when do we go after those bastards?" a sergeant shouted, referring to the Krauts opposite us. As I was responding, "Soon, I hope," a bullet zinged by my head, apparently from the rifle of a German sniper who had crawled forward in the darkness. All of us dropped to the ground. My men had been instructed not to call me "Lieutenant" when the platoon was within hearing distance of the enemy, because their snipers were rewarded for killing American officers.

The company jeep couldn't get to this area, so during the night small groups went to the saddle to pick up C or K rations and fill their canteens with water. Mahlin and I took turns acting as guides.

Fog reduced visibility to 15 or 20 feet the next morning. The guys liked that because they were able to leave their foxholes, visit with each other, and wander about. I disliked it because although the Krauts couldn't see us, we couldn't see them either and German soldiers might emerge, weapons blazing, at any moment. "Don't worry," a squad leader remarked when I voiced concern, "the sentries are watching."

"Okay," I replied, giving him a thumbs up, but my concern remained. Nobody appeared and before long the fog lifted.

Mahlin acquired a gas burner five inches or so in diameter and eight or nine high, equipped with a small cylinder of propane. That noon we used a canteen cup to heat water on it for coffee, ate a C ration for lunch, then rested. Not able to relax, I strolled back to the saddle, talked awhile with Mulvaney, studied the north side of the knoll and the hill adjacent to it, saw no sign of activity, rejoined Mahlin, washed the dirt off my face, and shaved. Sporadic firing south of us was followed by continuous firing for half an hour or so.

At dusk a small, open-cockpit plane with German insignia on the fuselage flew by. "Who the hell is that?" I asked Mahlin. He didn't know. We learned later that it was a Kraut intelligence officer looking over our position. The old timers called him "Bed Check Charlie" because he did this almost every evening. Sometimes they fired at him; sometimes they simply waved.

Benson awakened me at 3 a.m., saying I was to report at once to Captain Kaznolwicz's CP. The other platoon leaders were examining a map, illuminated by flashlights, when I arrived. From a hill ahead of us, Kaz announced, the Krauts had an unobstructed view of the 101st's front lines. Our battalion was to seize this hill. My platoon would attack it from the north, Second and Third Platoons from the west, G Company from the south. We were to start forward when a 20-minute barrage by the division artillery ended at 0725. Mortars would drop shells on defending enemy troops until it was no longer possible to do so without endangering us. Machine guns would provide additional support. I marked on my map the unit designations, departure points and boundaries that were noted on his. Extra ammunition, Kaz told me, was being issued to all platoons. "Let's show 'em what we can do, Steve," he urged as I prepared to leave. "We will," I answered, pumped up by his exuberance, and took off for the knoll.

On my way to it I considered how the platoon ought to proceed. According to Kaz, a German battalion, probably not at full strength, held this area. To reach the hill, which was southeast of us, my men would have to pass in front of or drive back the ones facing us. As soon as the artillery barrage was over, I decided, First Squad, led by me, should run toward a small gully 75 yards east of our knoll, firing from the hip at the enemy position ahead while the other two squads covered us from their foxholes. We would then provide protective fire so Second Squad could advance to the gully; after that both squads would go forward. Mahlin, observing our progress, would determine when and where to commit Third Squad. Both he and the squad leaders, who had been summoned to the CP by Benson, agreed with this.

"Walt," I said when we were alone, "if First Squad gets wiped out, keep the other two here. Send word to company headquarters that we didn't make it and ask what you should do." He nodded and murmured, "Okay."

Half an hour later a medical corpsman arrived. "I'm assigned to your platoon, Lieutenant," he told me. "Good," I replied; but it seemed like poor psychology to have a medic nearby while we waited for our first attack to begin, so I asked him to stay back until after we departed. "These guys are brave," I thought, referring to the unarmed medics who accompany troops going into combat, and wondered how badly we would need one.

Daylight was filtering through haze on the eastern horizon when the barrage began. Mahlin and I walked along the line of foxholes our men had been in for two days, reminding them to stay spread out as they advanced and giving encouragement. None of them seemed to be afraid. Each realized, I suppose, that some would be wounded, perhaps killed, and hoped it would not happen to him. Most believed, probably — as did I — that whether you survived was up to God or else a matter of luck. If a bullet has your name on it, there's nothing you can do. A few, no doubt, yearned for a million dollar wound — one that results in lengthy hospitalization but doesn't cause permanent disability.

I recalled wondering, on the *Saturnia*, whether I had the courage and ability to lead the platoon against enemy soldiers. The answer, I now felt, was yes — though having never experienced combat, I couldn't be sure. We'd practiced attacks like this on maneuvers, but in them the machine guns and rifles fired blank cartridges and mortar shells were flour-filled paper sacks. Would real ones distract or unnerve me? I didn't think so, or anticipate that fear would cause me to waver, but courage on the battlefield must be tested and mine hadn't been.

The minutes crept by. Shell after shell exploded 300 yards in front of us. I glanced at my watch for the umpeenth time: 7:19. It passed through my mind as I waited, nervous and impatient, that I knew very little about these 40 men — how much education they'd had, what they did before entering the service, what they expected to do after the war. If some die, will it be my fault? When one of them, looking up from his foxhole, said, "We have faith in you, Lieutenant," my confidence soared.

The artillery stopped at 0725. "Be with me, Lord," I whispered, then shouted, "Okay, guys, let's go," and hoping at least a few would follow, ran forward.

No bullets came my way; the Krauts must be holding off until we got nearer. I zig-zagged in order to be a more difficult target to hit, reached the gully, flopped down, and looked around. First Squad, led by its sergeant, was close behind me; Second Squad had started in our direction. South of us, Dorgan's platoon was encountering heavy fire. We should help him, I decided, and giving the signal to advance sprinted ahead. The rat-a-tat-tat of automatic weapons immediately filled the air. Slugs from German burp guns whizzed past my ears. Several of my men fell, not injured, apparently, because they commenced firing from the prone position toward the hill. The rest ran, crawled or rolled to spots that offered protection. I headed for a large rock some farmer had conveniently left in his field, and crouching beside it considered whether we should keep going or, for the moment, stay put. We're doing all right, I concluded, in spite of the small arms fire coming our way; and determined not to be slowed by excessive caution, rushed on. A mortar shell, landing nearby, exploded; I felt the concussion, heard somebody cry out in pain, sensed that something had struck my leg, and waving for both squads to continue, kept running.

Bullets raked the area in front of me. I veered away from them, dove into a shallow furrow, and looked back. First Squad's leader was less than 15 yards to my rear, several of his men alongside him, the rest behind them. They had dropped down, waiting, apparently, to see what I did. Off to our left, Second Squad was taking cover. A medic, the red cross on his helmet clearly visible, raced to where someone was kneeling beside a twisted body. Ricocheting shrapnel made an eerie, banshee sound as it changed direction. The din of weapons firing, shells bursting and people shouting was deafening. Your job is to lead this platoon to victory, not get it slaughtered, I told myself; what's the smart thing to do now?

Several First Squad guys crawled up to me and began firing. A couple of them tossed hand grenades that detonated on the ground 100 feet ahead of us, sending up geysers of dirt, or exploded in the air, launching showers of jagged fragments. An injured Kraut, arms flailing, rose, stiffened and fell back.

Finally, one by one, soldiers in front of us left their foxholes and darted up the hill. My men brought down quite a few. This, I realized, was an ideal time for us to advance. Jumping up, I yelled, "Go," and dashed after them. An ashen-faced German lying on his back, blood gushing from a shoulder, looked at me with terror in his eyes. I kicked away his burp gun and went on. Second Squad men began firing from abandoned foxholes at Krauts on the summit; others, shielded by the brow of the hill, edged forward. Third Squad was on its way toward us from the knoll.

Suddenly the hilltop became a mass of people withdrawing to the east. All of us surged ahead. So did the rest of Company E, attacking from the west. Gray and I reached the crest of the hill at the same time. A moment later O'Neal showed up. "Stay here," he barked. "G Company will be on the south slope. A counterattack is expected." Without waiting for us to reply or ask questions, he raced off.

The squad leaders began assembling their men. Mahlin arrived, joined them and pointed to where they should go. Removing my canteen for a swallow of water, I discovered that it was empty, punctured by a bullet.

Benson, materializing out of nowhere, said, "I lost you, Lieutenant." It flashed through my mind that this would be impossible if he was near me, as he should have been, since I (like most front-line lieutenants) had a white stripe on the back of my helmet to help advancing soldiers spot their platoon leader. Had Benson tarried on purpose?

"My God, sir, you're hurt," he exclaimed, noticing my leg. I'd completely forgotten about it. Through a rip in my pants we could see, on the side of one calf, a bloody three-inch slash half an inch deep, apparently caused by shrapnel. He sprinkled sulfa powder from his first aid packet on it and applied a bandage while I talked with Gray, who informed me that Dorgan, hit in the face by a shell fragment, had been taken to the rear. Where Kaz and Albertson were he didn't know. Jud, scouting around in the dark before our attack started, got shot in the groin by a sentry who mistook him for an infiltrator. The wound, though not life-threatening, was painful and might affect his virility.

Mahlin came over with a report on casualties. Seven of our

men had injuries. Three were being treated by medics, the other four by doctors at the battalion aid station. I was amazed that so few had been wounded, and none killed, since bullets and shrapnel were everywhere. The fact that "everywhere" included a great deal of empty space must be the reason.

"Did anybody hold back?" I asked.

"I don't think so," Mahlin replied. "Some hesitated but went on when they saw those ahead advancing."

"Good," I said; then, putting my helmet on the ground, sat on it, rinsed the dirt out of my mouth with water from his canteen, drank a little, used some to wash the grimy sweat from my eyes, and resting there, still breathing hard from the exertion, realized that not once during the entire attack did I fire my carbine. Although this wasn't anything to be ashamed of – after all, I hadn't been standing around enjoying the scenery – it embarrassed me. So did not killing the wounded German I ran past. That probably was something to be ashamed of; next time I mustn't be so tender-hearted.

A medic examined my leg wound, cleaned it, taped the skin together, and replaced the bandage. The battalion S-3 arrived to check our deployment and find out what the platoon needed. "Ammunition," I told him, not knowing whether we really did; subconsciously recalling, perhaps, the captain's advice to submit requisitions even if you have to lie.

Heavy fighting was taking place a mile or so to the south. I couldn't see much, notwithstanding the hill's commanding view, but noise from that direction pounded my eardrums. A small town seemed to be burning up; black smoke rose above it and flames were visible. I wondered what was happening there.

The anticipated counterattack came that afternoon. Riflemen approaching from the east through a small forest subjected our position to relentless fire. We returned it from foxholes dug by them or their comrades, grateful for the protection. A company on its way to support us hit the attacking force's flank. Machine guns sent to help G Company added to our firepower. It appeared that the Krauts, despite heavy casualties, were not going to withdraw, but they finally did. Three more of my privates and two non-coms were injured. The others, as I walked among them, looked tired. No jubilation was evident. Several, seeking reassurance, asked, "Did we do okay?"

That evening I thought about the day's events. Whether our success had been due to luck, courage or skill was unclear; some of each, maybe. Regarding one thing there could be no question: First Platoon's soldiers had performed well. They didn't hesitate or hug the ground in fear but instead advanced bravely and made commendable use of individual initiative. Mahlin's timing in committing our reserve squad and his subsequent maneuvering of it were excellent. My men had been tested in battle – baptized by fire – and emerged triumphant.

And I? – had I performed well, or at least satisfactorily? Yes; I, too, moved forward in the face of enemy fire, showed initiative, and though scared, let fear play no role in my decisions. It was probably wise for me to be out in front, since this was our initial attack, but in the future it might be desirable to stay farther back, where, having a better view, I could exercise more effective control. Not very far back, though, because in the confusion of combat, orders must be communicated by arm and hand signals or shouting. Also, to succeed, platoon leaders must be with their men.

The amount of protection level ground provided surprised me. It wasn't really level, of course; there were furrows, hollows, shell holes, stone walls, ditches, rocks like the one I came across, here and there a tree stump, and what our OCS field manuals referred to as defilade – the protection that even a slight rise or indentation gives against flying bullets and shrapnel. Mother Earth, except when she is mined or her grass and shrubs conceal booby traps, is an infantryman's friend; his foxhole is akin to the womb.

The next day troops from another battalion replaced us. We trudged through pouring rain to a valley previously occupied by Krauts, huddled in their trenches and vacated gun emplacements until the following morning, then marched to a wooded area some three miles distant where Kaz rejoined the company. In a letter written after the war he described what kept him away:

When the platoons neared the top of the hill, I started forward with the command post group – the first sergeant, my radio man, my two runners, an observer from the field artillery, and two field artillery radio men. Halfway up the hill a shell landed at my feet. It took me up into the air. I came down head first. Before hitting the ground my helmet got turned sideways. It cut my scalp badly and knocked me cold. I received no shrapnel but the others did: my radio man in the shins, the FA guy in the knees, the two FA radio men in the thighs, our top sergeant in the hips, and the two runners in the chest. Both of them died.

When the medics saw my wound they assumed it was more serious and left me for dead. I was not evacuated until dusk. At the hospital they patched me up. I ate well and was sent back the next day. It was raining cats and dogs. Col. Scott took me to where there were about 30 men. They'd had no sleep and everybody was wet. He pointed to a little town on his map and said to go to it and rest, that there weren't any enemy soldiers there. By then it was late afternoon. He drew a line to the town on his map with a grease pencil. The rain splattered on it and the width of the grease pencil line covered about half a mile. I was confused and didn't know where O'Neal was or E Company or any other outfit.

In the rain and darkness we had to feel for the road. When we thought we were near the town we got in a huddle for a discussion and noticed two strangers who turned out to be Germans on guard duty. We surprised them and made them lead us into town, then divided into two groups, with a German in each group, and went to each house very quietly and captured the Germans in their beds. It went like clockwork. We got the company commander and also I got his car, an old Chrysler. Later I had my serial number stenciled on the bumper. It stayed with the kitchen train and the supply sergeant drove it.

At the far end of town the road crossed a stream. There was a mill on the other side of it. There were no civilians in town. We thought we had all the German soldiers and put them inside the mill. I posted guards and everybody else, including me, went to sleep in the houses. When someone woke me up the sun was shining. He pointed out a window. A German tank was in the road by the mill. A German soldier who'd been hiding ran over and yelled something to the tank commander. He right away pulled down the hatch, turned the tank around and headed back to where he'd come from. All of us started firing at the tank but it didn't do any good. We hauled a large wagon across the road to block it. I walked up the hill to look around and found a group of Yugoslavians in funny pea green uniforms. They were laborers and happy to surrender, hoping to be sent to the States.

This action all happened because Col. Scott said there were no enemy troops in the town. We killed one German and got 75 prisoners – did all of this with 30 tired wet soldiers, no map, no radio, no heavy weapons, no U. S. casualties, just a lot of guts.

O'Neal warned us that the Krauts were using our passwords. I learned later how they acquired them. One night a YD sentry heard somebody and called out "Halt." Receiving no answer he moved forward to investigate, whereupon a German who spoke English called "Halt" to him. The sentry responded with the initial word, to which the German replied, "O.K." Assuming it was an American, the sentry returned to his post. The next time the German was challenged he answered with the initial word and received in reply the second word. This, the 26th Division History says, permitted him to scout behind our lines "unmolested."

Although Patton's armored divisions were handicapped by a shortage of fuel, they and his infantry divisions continued to fight, pushing ahead to improve unit alignments, eliminate pockets, seize strategic locations, and ward off counterattacks by Nazi commanders determined to regain territory formerly held. An article in the *New York Times* reported that the 26th Division was encountering "fanatical, bitter-end resistance. ... American dough-boys are fighting and dying on this side of the Moselle."

Kaz, full of enthusiasm, returned from a briefing at regimental headquarters with information about another attack. "Your platoon gets to take this village," he told me, pointing on his map to a cluster of 15 or so tiny squares that represented buildings. "Three tanks are being assigned to us. You can follow them down the road." That sounded good; it would be nice to advance behind huge hunks of armor – unless, of course, tank destroyers were waiting to blast them. "Great," I replied; but walking back to my CP I realized that this wasn't how I really felt. Divine Providence may have protected a few in our first attack, but most of us lived through it because we were lucky. Things might well be different next time. The longer we continued fighting, the more likely death became. I wished our regiment could go to the rear and be held in reserve. What I wanted most of all was for the war to end; and I suspected that my men, despite their bravery, yearned for this too.

The tanks didn't show up but we went down the road anyway, since its ditches furnished protection, Second squad on the left, First and Third Squads on the right, each of them spread out in single file. Mahlin and I, at the head of the column, kept our eyes peeled for activity in the village and the land adjacent to it but saw none. That concerned me. The enemy's outposts and weapons must be well concealed. Are there soldiers inside the houses? Hiding behind them? Kneeling in foxholes we haven't spotted? 300 yards or so from the edge of town I halted the platoon and sent three men through the fields to our left and three through those to our right with instructions to look around. One group, crossing a small rise, dropped out of sight; a grove of trees swallowed up the others. I watched anxiously as the rest of us moved slowly forward.

All of a sudden a member of the second group appeared on the road where it entered the village and signalled for us to come on. No Krauts were present, only a handful of French who waved from doorways as we passed by. "They don't seem glad to see us," Mahlin remarked. I agreed; there were no American flags, no hand-clasps or cheers, no cups of wine or cider like those we received in Normandy. Perhaps German troops here had treated them well; the houses appeared to be undamaged. Perhaps Third Army units occupied this area earlier and treated them poorly; the front line had see-sawed back and forth. "These people have a Kraut heritage," our sniper commented; "maybe they didn't want to be liberated."

My orders were to keep going, so we did, to a highway several miles beyond, where Kaz met us. Our opposition, he said, had withdrawn. Although that was a relief, it was frustrating, too, because we were emotionally ready for this encounter and let down by its failure to materialize. The only way to get the war over with was to eliminate as many Germans as possible. I had visualized us surrounding the town and capturing its defenders. The unexpected withdrawal made this impossible.

Not everything turned out well for YD. The captain commanding an enemy company reported to his superiors a successful counterattack against 26th Division personnel:

> *Artillery, anti-tank guns and mortar fire grew more violent, and in the afternoon the Americans attacked. My Company was driven out of the trenches on hill 265 due west of Bezange la Petite and defended itself from houses in the village. I planned with Panzer platoon leader Lt. Rudolph a counter attack. When daylight broke, we started with 3 Panzer IV's accompanied by an infantry assault force. Shooting, throwing hand grenades, and shouting loudly we stormed toward hill 265 and were successful. The enemy retreated and we were again in possession of our former position. Approximately 15 noncommissioned officers and soldiers were taken prisoner.*

A YD lieutenant described how his platoon was "tricked" by three Krauts who approached with their hands up. Excited by the opportunity to take prisoners, some of his men ran toward them. "The exposed Germans dropped down and a curtain of rifle and automatic weapons fire sprayed our line of march. We captured some prisoners, but we surely learned a lesson the hard way."

On October 11th my three squads were in foxholes on the forward slope of a small hill. Mahlin and I had our CP halfway up the reverse slope. In army jargon, forward slope means the side facing the enemy; the side away from them is the reverse slope. Benson and three others were behind us where they could watch for patrols that might try to sneak into our position. The rest of 2nd Battalion – all but my platoon – was on a ridge some 50 yards to our rear. The Germans occupied a similar ridge 400 yards east of us. Nothing seemed to be happening, so I fished a sheet of paper out of my musette bag and began a letter to the folks – my first since we left Normandy. No mail had been delivered to us. I attempted to tell them, in a way the censor wouldn't catch on to, that the division had joined Patton's Third Army and that we were in combat. "War is hell," the closing sentence declared, quoting General Sherman. I was addressing an envelope when Kaz called on the telephone – a line had been laid from his CP to mine. "O'Neal wants to know how many Krauts are in Xanrey and the gun emplacements they have," he said. "Go there as soon as it gets dark and see what you can find out."

The village of Xanrey – 18 or 20 structures along a narrow country road – was half a mile southeast of us. I studied the terrain between it and our position, decided on a route to follow, noted landmarks that would serve as guides, looked for obstacles to avoid, then picked two men, Sabatini and Kinzer, to take along and gave them instructions: "We'll leave at 1900 hours. Wear your field jacket inside out so it won't reflect moonlight or make a noise if you brush against something. Wear a stocking cap instead of your helmet for the same reason. Keep your wrist watch concealed so its luminous face doesn't disclose our presence. Don't bring your rifle or bayonet; they catch on fences, scrape against rocks, and trip booby trap wires. Each of us will have a grenade for emergency use. Talk only when it's necessary to and only in whispers. Remember the password."

Rain was falling at 7, so I postponed our departure. At 9, despite the continuing downpour, we started toward Xanrey. No landmarks were visible, nor was anything else. I proceeded entirely by compass, cupping my hands around the dial to prevent it from serving as a beacon. Not knowing whether we were on or off course worried me, and I wondered who or what we might come face to face with on the next step. At fences I ran a hand gingerly along the wires and between them for evidence of booby traps, then rolled carefully under the lowest strand, followed by the other two. We encountered things I hadn't expected: sunflowers that towered above our heads, a creek not shown on my map or noticeable when I looked over the area, a tall, lattice-like structure that turned out to be a grape arbor, a low stone wall overgrown with weeds, a potato patch that added layers of mud to our boots as we slithered through it, and innumerable fences, far more than I knew existed. Were we, perhaps, lost? The others had compasses, too; we paused frequently to check them. Occasionally we stopped because of unfamiliar noises, listened intently, then went on.

Kinzer's knee struck a rock when his foot slipped and he fell. "Can you keep going?" I asked. Waiting there until Sabatini and I returned, or making his way back alone, were the only other choices, I felt. "I"ll stay with you," he replied; "I can make it." We started forward, hoping nobody had heard his cry of pain.

Suddenly something loomed up less than five feet in front of me. I recognized it as one of the small buildings at the edge of Xanrey. A house should be next. We crept ahead and came to it. The windows were dark. Are enemy riflemen inside, or in nearby foxholes? Are they watching us? Are sentries posted around the corner or behind trees? Telling Sabatini and Kinzer to wait, I stole silently forward to the muddy road – Xanrey's main street, Xanrey's only street. There was no sign of life, no evidence of weapons emplacements, no sound except the rain cascading down in torrents. It occurred to me that determining the number of German soldiers in Xanrey would be impossible; they were either in the houses or holed up someplace else. Why risk getting two men and myself killed or captured? Also, headquarters wanted my report no later than 4 a.m. It was 12:30, so we'd already been gone three and a half hours. Returning to the others I said, "We've done enough. Let's head for home." There was no dissent.

The trip back took less time. I left Sabatini and Kinzer at the base of our hill, located the battalion command post, gave the S-2 what little information I'd gathered, then trudged through the darkness to my foxhole, where I discovered that one side of it had caved in, burying my blankets, helmet, carbine, canteen and musette bag. I wanted to cry out in dismay – the patrol had been so miserable, and now this – but instead curled up on the rain-soaked ground and, exhausted, slept.

An approaching artillery shell woke me. Unable to use my own foxhole I rolled into Mahlin's, knocking the breath out of him and, he told me later, scaring him "shitless."

At 0500, moving along our forward slope to check on the men, I heard a voice say, "Mama, Mama, help me, I'm afraid." My efforts to track it down led to the discovery that our sentries and the NCO on duty were dozing. I roused them, announced that they would be disciplined, and discussed with Mahlin what action to take. We decided to explain how this endangered everybody and threaten court martial if it happened again. Not much else could be done, we felt, without involving higher headquarters, which neither of us favored. Who called "Mama, Mama," remained a mystery. Perhaps he did it unconsciously, in a dream.

By mid-morning, the rain had stopped. I retrieved my gear, repaired my foxhole, cleaned my carbine, and shaved in case Patton dropped by. It seemed unlikely that he would – generals hardly ever came this close to the front – but one couldn't be sure and it had been made clear that Old Blood and Guts accepted no excuses.

I wondered what his other divisions were doing. How many does he have? Is 4th Armored in action? I had no idea what was taking place in the First Army sector north of us, or in southern France, Italy or the Pacific. Mother, listening to newscasters on her radio and reading the local newspaper, knew far more than I.

That evening a Second Squad rifleman claimed to be sick. Convinced of his sincerity, I sent him to the aid station and considered whether the physical discomforts my guys were enduring might be wearing them out. They'd had no hot food for nearly three weeks, their clothes were almost always wet or damp, it was cold, and we'd been in sight of the enemy most of the time, not back where greater opportunities for relaxation arose. Leaving their foxholes in daylight exposed them to snipers and mortar shells; after dark, to German patrols. Both Mahlin and I, while checking on them at night, had been fired at by unseen Krauts who heard our voices.

Maybe they weren't getting enough sleep. Maybe I wasn't either. Rifle shots half a mile away or a far-off burst of machine gun fire or distant artillery repeatedly awakened me. So did messages from unit commanders and intelligence officers, their pre-dawn meetings, or the arrival of our food and water even though Sgt. Mulvaney supervised its distribution. Attempts at sleep during the day rarely succeeded.

We'd been warned about trenchfoot and were required to change sox regularly. Although the wet ones didn't dry out before we put them on again, none of us had been incapacitated.

Everybody in the platoon got plenty to eat, but C and K rations lose their appeal after awhile. The Quartermaster was supposed to furnish a variety of K rations, which came in a small box made of paraffin-treated cardboard, but those I received were almost always the same: cheese, a little can of meat, two fruit bars, powdered coffee, chocolate, and a pack of four cigarettes. C rations consisted of a can of beef stew, pork and beans, or something similar, and a separate can containing crackers, packets of powdered coffee or lemonade, sugar cubes and hard candy.

No one had complained, at least not to me, but none of this was pleasant or good for morale.

The following day blue sky appeared and the sun began to shine. I let its rays warm my body and was napping when Kaz showed up on our hill. "The Krauts have an outpost 75 yards in front of their position," he told me. "Organize a combat patrol, Steve, and drive them away. Capture one if you can. Then come back." A "concealed route" would allow us to get there without being seen. Some lieutenant from another battalion received a medal for leading a similar attack, he added enthusiastically; maybe I'd be given one, too.

Irregularities in the terrain ahead of us would hide soldiers crawling on their stomachs, and undergrowth in the fields might provide additional concealment; he was right about that. But plenty of open places existed, too, including our forward slope and the land on either side of it. "There isn't any concealed route, Kaz," I replied. He wanted to see for himself and headed up the hill, crouching at first, then on his hands and knees, while Mahlin and I discussed who should go with me. Kaz returned and readily accepted my suggestion that we look things over from the higher ground at our rear. On the way to it he criticized Lt. Albertson for rarely leaving his foxhole and for requesting hospitalization on account of battle fatigue.

O'Neal, hidden by shrubs, was looking through a tripod-mounted telescope. "Keep down," he warned, then slid aside so I could study the enemy ridge and a knoll that projected out from it toward us. We talked for a couple of minutes. "Take this," he said, handing me an automatic rifle commonly referred to as a grease gun. It was the only infantry weapon I knew nothing about, but I appreciated his generosity, since they were hard to acquire, and had no doubts concerning my ability to make effective use of it if necessary. "Kill as many as you can," Kaz urged, "but try to get a prisoner."

I described our mission to the ten men selected by Mahlin and gave them instructions. We moved out in diamond formation, going slowly and quietly to preserve the element of surprise. Night had fallen but their shadowy figures behind me and the outline of trees on top of the distant enemy ridge were visible. Knowing that patrols, scouts or snipers might be anywhere, I peered warily in all directions. Eventually the blurry, black mass of the ridge came into view. We were creeping forward when, north of us, on the projecting knoll, I saw what appeared to be the silhouette of a man and realized from the shape of his helmet that it was a German soldier. Another one joined him. I rotated my body 90 degrees in order to face that way; signalled "Down" to the patrol, which was now to my left; and as the two figures started toward us, debated what to do. Should we attempt to capture them, or would this reveal our presence to occupants of the nearby outpost and their comrades up on the ridge? Before I could decide, a member of my patrol shouted "Halt!" Remembering Kaz's admonition to "kill as many as you can," I raised the grease gun to my shoulder, aimed at the approaching pair, and pressed the trigger. One of them fell, the other turned and ran. My men immediately began firing. So did Krauts on the knoll. Noise and muzzle flashes filled the air for a minute or so, then stopped. I was considering whether to advance when the sound of somebody gasping for breath distracted me. It was important, I concluded, to re-establish contact with the patrol before doing anything.

Several of them were gathered around Korinek, who, wounded in the legs, was writhing in pain. I told Corporal Murphy to get him to our aid station and stated that I would bring his rifle; battalion headquarters had notified us that they were in short supply and shouldn't be abandoned. "We have a prisoner," Moeller called to me. "He was in this hole, too scared to resist."

A low, gurgling noise drifted through the darkness. I crawled quickly in that direction and reached Thompson, lying face-up on the ground. The noise had stopped. "Can you hear me?" I asked, kneeling beside him. He didn't answer. I touched his cheek. No response. Applying a finger to his wrist, I detected a faint throbbing but was unsure whether it came from the beating of his heart or the pounding of mine. I listened for the sound of breathing, my ear next to his nose and mouth. Nothing. I slid my hand under his shirt to check for heartbeat. When it went through what felt like thick, warm pudding, I realized with horror that bullets had torn open his chest and my fingers were descending into his lungs. There was no reaction of any kind. This is how life ends on the battlefield, a voice within me whispered: the broken body gasps, struggles, gurgles and dies. I wanted to say I'm sorry or God bless you, even though he wouldn't hear me, or pat his arm as a gesture of farewell, but instead picked up the rifle lying beside him and stole away. German troops were close by and might strike at any moment. Sentiment would have to wait.

Returning to where the rest had gathered, I sent two men to our lines with the prisoner. Murphy and three others, carrying Korinek, had already left. A potato masher grenade flew over my head but exploded beyond us and did no harm.

The hole our prisoner had been in was big enough for ten people and contained blankets, clothes and gas masks. This was their outpost; the two I fired at apparently were going to it.

I couldn't find Korinek's rifle in the dark and didn't think wandering around alone this near the enemy was very smart, so I caught up with Sabatini and Polk, who were pulling Thompson's body away, and helped them drag it to some trees. We returned to our hill, where I described to Mahlin what had taken place.

Polk suggested that we go back "and get more Krauts." Sabatini and I, eager to avenge Thompson's death, agreed. We discussed how to proceed: inspect the outpost first, perhaps, then crawl up the knoll and lob grenades into the foxholes of the soldiers occupying it. The other two became less enthusiastic as we talked and proposed waiting "until tomorrow." I told them we should at least try to determine how many were there.

The three of us set out, following an indirect route which provided greater concealment. When recognizable landmarks disappeared and the terrain changed, it became clear that we had gone too far and were near a different part of the knoll. Less enthusiastic myself by then, I decided to head for our lines, but in a roundabout manner so as not to inadvertently penetrate the German position. We moved stealthily through a wooded area, watching for their patrols or one of our own that might mistake us for Krauts. Clouds kept the moon and stars from serving as guides; trees obscured the outline of First Platoon's hill and the high ground behind it. I was worried about getting lost in this unfamiliar section of no-man's-land when we unexpectedly came upon Thompson's body. That gave us our bearings.

I reported to Kaz by telephone, informing him that the knoll, which supposedly was unoccupied, appeared to be a segment of the enemy's main line of resistance; then, psychologically and physically drained, lay down and was almost asleep when the phone buzzed. Mahlin answered. "It's the captain, calling for you."

"Is a rifle missing?" Kaz asked. I said yes.

"Did you search for it?"

"I did some, Kaz; I tried to. Three of us went back but we lost our way. We got to the base of the knoll."

"Better try again, Steve. Pick up Korinek's rifle and look around."

"Okay," I replied wearily; another trip to that area was the last thing in the world I wanted. Kaz must have sensed this, because he added: "Now don't take any chances. Just a little reconnaissance patrol to see if everybody has left the outpost. And get that gun, and bring us one of theirs if you can."

I found Benson and asked him to go with me. "I can't, sir; I'm too upset by what's happened," he replied.

"Everybody's upset," I said. "Grab your rifle and let's go."

"Don't make me, Lieutenant, please don't; I can't do it," he pleaded.

Angered by this lack of cooperation and unexpected display of cowardice, I considered ordering him to come, but didn't. Turning away in disgust, I located Sabatini and Polk. "A man is not a machine," my report at Fort Jackson had stated; he must have "sufficient rest to keep his mind and senses keen and alert." These guys shouldn't be going out there a third time and neither should I, but that's what we were about to do. Maybe in combat you didn't follow the book.

We took our weapons – this wasn't according to the book either, since it was "just a little reconnaissance patrol," but having them appeared to be wise – and once again moved cautiously through the night, alert for enemy soldiers who might be hiding nearby or quietly stealing forward. When a dead branch I stepped on noisily snapped in two, we instinctively dropped down. Nothing happened. On the ridge the flame from a cigarette being lighted flickered momentarily. South of us an automatic rifle fired half a dozen bursts.

One person makes less noise than three and is less likely to attract attention, so when we were 50 yards from the outpost I told the other two to wait while I sneaked ahead to see if it had been reoccupied. If nobody was there we would search for Korinek's rifle and scout around.

The best way to approach an outpost is from the rear; its occupants usually won't be watching in that direction, and if they hear a noise may believe it came from their own troops. The open tract our combat patrol had been in seemed ideal for this. I crept through it as silently as possible, then on my stomach started toward the hole. Scared now, fearful that a German soldier with his gun pointed in my direction was waiting for me to get closer, I inched ahead, pausing frequently to listen, glancing over my shoulder from time to time to be sure nobody was coming, more than once thinking, "Why am I doing this?" – the mission didn't seem that important. Expecting a muzzle flash at any moment, followed by bullets ramming into my face, I longed to go back but forced myself to keep on.

Something caused me to turn my head, some noise, perhaps, or a sixth sense or fear or habit. What I saw made my heart stop. Eight Krauts were standing behind me with raised rifles. One of them put his knee on my neck and grabbed the grease gun. "Oh my God," I thought; "what have I done!"

6

The guy with his knee on me removed it. Uncertain whether those raised rifles were about to be fired, I rolled over very slowly and sat up, then got to my feet. Someone spoke. "Don't understand," I responded. Another tried. Recognizing the word "blessure," I decided he was asking in French about wounds and shook my head.

"Kameraden?"

We'd learned that Kraut soldiers, when surrounded, often came out of their foxholes, with hands up, shouting "Kamerad" to indicate surrender. Now the tables were turned. "Ja, ja, Kamerad," I affirmed; being their prisoner was better than being shot. This didn't satisfy him and words continued to pour forth. I finally realized that he wanted to know whether I had comrades and answered, "Nein," thinking for the first time of Sabatini and Polk. Can they see or hear what's happening?

My captors talked briefly, then one of them stepped around and put the muzzle of his rifle against my spine. "Jesus, they really are going to kill me," I murmured, bracing myself, but their leader signalled that I was to follow him and started toward the knoll. Somebody, grabbing an arm, yanked me forward. A muzzle remained between my shoulder blades.

The remorse I'd felt while standing there became overwhelming as we walked along in silence. Only flight – running from the enemy in terror – was more despicable than capture. I had failed the platoon, let down my company and battalion, negated months of training. How could I have been so careless, so stupid?

Halfway up the knoll a column of soldiers going to the outpost passed us. At the top, dozens of others were lounging beside foxholes. Cigarette smoke filled the air; its unique aroma was a pungent reminder that these were enemy troops.

After pausing a minute or two while they conferred with a Feldwebel, we headed toward the ridge. I watched for anti-tank guns, heavy weapons and concentrations of personnel – information that might be valuable to our S-2 – and thought about escaping. A hand grenade in my pocket had been overlooked; perhaps I could slip it out, pull the pin, toss it at those behind me and run. Run where? Getting to our lines would be impossible, I concluded, and unnecessarily risking death seemed foolish.

We came to what probably was their battalion CP. People were lying on the ground, some awake, some sleeping. A different person searched me and found the grenade. Four men – presumably officers – showed up and carried on a conversation in German. As they were leaving, one said in a friendly but condescending voice, "Sit down, boy." I did, and at once discovered that this particular spot was muddy. Weary and discouraged, I decided to endure a wet bottom rather than move.

Two guards stayed with me. After awhile, changing positions because my rear was thoroughly soaked, I inadvertently exposed the luminous dial of my wrist watch. They immediately seized it. "You sons of bitches," I said, but recalled that my soldiers had done the same with our prisoner a few hours earlier.

Instructions arrived and we departed. Three of them took me across fields, under barbed wire fences, along a highway where lots of riflemen were waiting, and ultimately into a house. A Kraut NCO at a switchboard appeared to be unnerved by my presence. That provided a little encouragement: it proved they weren't supermen.

Twenty minutes later I was put in the back seat of a dilapidated old car. A guard sat beside me; another by the man who drove. We went along a country road, with lights off because the front lines were not far away. Our ride, under different circumstances, would have been hilarious; it was likc a Laurel and Hardy movie. The guard by the driver rode with his head out the window, squinting into the darkness. When the car started into the ditch on the right he would shout, "Links, Links, Links"; when it approached the other side he yelled, "Rechts, Rechts, Rechts." Back and forth we lurched, sometimes going half way down the embankment, occasionally coming to a complete stop. Finally the driver failed to "Links" quickly enough; we struck a cement culvert, lost a wheel, and ended up in the ditch. Following a brief discussion, they led me through an open area to a series of fortifications I assumed were part of the Maginot Line.

Except for scattered sentries, there was no sign of life. Every so often one guard would disappear down steps leading to underground bunkers, then reappear and go on. Eventually he found the right spot and beckoned to me. We descended into a room about 12 feet square, constructed of poured concrete. A wood-burning stove provided warmth and gave off a little light. People were sleeping in bunks along the walls. Somebody, rising up on an elbow, asked in English, "You are from the one-o-four regiment?"

"I can state nothing but my name, rank and serial number," I replied, scared but determined to be uncooperative.

He shrugged. "You will not be paid or receive any mail unless you tell us your regiment and home address." I didn't answer, but felt that if no pay and no letters from the family were the only consequences of being a prisoner, I needn't worry. After speaking to the guard, he said to me, "Our army has a place where they will make you talk," and without waiting for my reaction pulled the blanket over his head. That sounded more ominous. I had no idea what Kraut interrogators did to captured front-line officers. None of my training had prepared me for this.

We left the bunker, returned to the main road, and walked along it in silence. The eastern sky remained dark, the night air cold. I guessed it must be close to 5 a.m. Once, to our rear, the sound of small arms fire broke the stillness; I turned around but saw nothing.

An hour or so later we came to a cliff that rose straight up.

There was a wooden door in it which the first guard entered. He emerged in a few minutes, followed by a young lieutenant wearing a garrison coat, jodhpurs, highly-polished boots, an officer's dress hat, and a leather holster with a pistol in it. "This guy looks like he just graduated from OCS," I commented to myself.

The contrast between us must have been striking: he in his immaculate uniform, I clad in a dirty field jacket over an olive drab sweater and shirt, muddy pants that clung to my legs, a GI knit cap, and no insignia of rank. His face, in the dim pre-dawn light, seemed boyish, almost cherubic, and showed no sign of animosity or belligerence.

It soon became apparent that neither of us spoke the other's language. After hearing me say "I don't understand," half a dozen times, he opened the door and pointed inside.

The room was the size of the previous one and, like it, had bunks along the walls. These, however, were empty. A candle furnished the only light. We sat down at a table and he offered me a German cigarette, which I accepted. Nodding to indicate my appreciation, I removed from my shirt pocket a K ration pack of four Chesterfields and pulled one part way out for him. He took it, and striking a match lit both mine and his. We smoked awhile, then I pushed the package toward him. He slid the candle nearer to study the brand name, smiled, and said, "Shestafield."

"Ja, ja," I answered, and handing him the pack added, in English, "Here, for you." Pleased, he placed in front of me a plate heaped high with slices of dark bread. I ate several while he puffed on another cigarette. My last meal had been a can of unheated stew the previous noon.

Two soldiers came for me on a motorcycle. One drove; the other sat behind him. I rode in the side car, crouched down to escape the cold and be protected in event of a second encounter with the ditch. Just before daybreak we arrived at a partially demolished chateau. I was guided into a good-sized room and seated at a rectangular table that had six chairs around it. An officer perched on the edge of a bunk was pulling on his boots. He paid no attention to me, nor did the occupants of two other bunks, who were yawning and stretching. I laid my arms on the table top, rested my head on them and faded away.

The guy with the boots was slicing a sausage when my eyes opened; his comrades were dressing. All three acted as if I didn't exist. Pretty soon they brought food to the table, and while eating it conversed in loud voices and listened to music on a radio. At last, one of them, without saying a word, gave me some bread and a cup of coffee; then he and the others moved to nearby desks.

My heart grew heavy. I thought about the platoon. Will they get along all right? Will Polk and Sabatini know why I didn't return? Will Mother and Dad be told I was captured or just that I'm missing? Who notifies them? How quickly?

An orchestra seemed to be playing a song that was popular during my college days, Artie Shaw's arrangement of *Dancing In The Dark.* That worried me; I must be hallucinating, losing touch with reality. Had I been drugged? Is that why these men haven't spoken to me? Worry turned to consternation; if I'd been drugged, anything could happen. How do I handle this; what should I do? Then it dawned on me that those familiar strains were coming from the officers' radio.

Finally, one of them said, "Where are you from?"

"I cannot tell you. I am permitted to give only my name, rank and serial number."

"But that is so foolish, for without a home address we are unable to inform your family that you are safe." I remained silent.

"Which regiment were you in?" I shook my head.

He asked what I did prior to entering the service; I said I had been a student. A student, he replied, would understand that there wasn't any harm in responding to simple questions like these.

Before long another officer came in, offered me a cigarette, and explained that "after certain preliminaries" I would be sent to a prisoner of war camp. He wanted to know my hometown, my regiment and how much I was paid. I told him I lived in Lincoln, Nebraska, and the amount of my pay, but not the identity of my regiment. "America should be fighting the Russians instead of us," he remarked, and terminated the interview.

At noon a man in civilian clothes who claimed to be a Red Cross representative arrived. I was suspicious and said very little. When he left, the officer who'd done the initial questioning sat down opposite me and asked if my regiment was the 104th. I refused to answer. He persisted; worn out, I answered no. Apparently that satisfied him; he gave me some cigarettes and returned to his desk.

Was it wrong, I wondered, to disclose where I lived, how much the army paid me, and that I didn't belong to the 104th? Yes, I concluded; next time I must be more careful and not let weariness weaken my resolve.

They fed me a good meal at noon. I ate most of it, then got up, went over to a bunk, lay down and, exhausted, immediately fell asleep.

It was still light out when somebody roused me. An automobile ride followed. Feeling that escape might be possible I noted highway numbers, distances, and the names of towns but had trouble keeping them in mind. At a farm occupied by German soldiers my guards and I were served soup, after which we drove until late at night. In the residential area of a fairly large town the driver walked back and forth along a street searching for the right house. When he found it I was released to guards there. They took me along a hallway to a padlocked door. One of them opened it and pushed me into a room where three brown-skinned people, wearing turbans, were sitting on a straw-covered floor. The door closed and the lock snapped shut. My efforts to communicate with the other occupants failed. I gave each of them a cigarette and smoked one myself.

At dawn the four of us were put in the cargo bed of a truck. Upon reaching our destination, several hours later, I was led to a barn filled with U. S. enlisted men, including sixteen YD's who, a sergeant explained, were captured because the ammunition clips issued to them didn't fit their rifles. We received no breakfast but at noon had goulash, then were transported in trucks to Saverne. The following morning two guards and I boarded a train and rode in a passenger coach full of Krauts. Many of them stared at me, some out of curiosity, some with hostility. One, sneering, spit on my jacket. I stood up but was yanked back by the soldier guarding me, who unceremoniously shoved the guy away. We got off at Strasbourg. After waiting in the rain for almost an hour, watched by a policeman who kept the muzzle of his revolver in my back the entire time, I was taken to a warehouse, searched, and handed a postcard to mail home reporting my new status: P.O.W. I hesitated, concerned that identifying the folks might subject them to harrassment by Nazi agents in the U.S., but decided that this was foolish, wrote their names and address on the front, and fervently hoped it would arrive before a "missing in action" notification did.

My next stop was a building four or five stories in height. Accompanied by a guard, I climbed three flights of stairs and went to a room where seven American officers were seated around a table. "Come in," one of them called out cheerily.

They were about my age and had been captured recently. Five were infantrymen; the other two, Air Corps pilots. Food, they stated, was brought once a day, in the afternoon: bread, sometimes a little meat or cheese, and occasionally potatoes. The adjoining room had cots for sleeping and there was a latrine near the stairway.

"Aren't these doors locked?" I asked.

"Just the one to the building. We're the only people here. This is a hospital the Krauts abandoned because it's close to a bridge over the Rhine that is frequently bombed. You can scout around if you want to."

Our chow came at three o'clock: two loaves of bread for us to divide equally, margarine, a bit of jam, and a large container of hot coffee. "It's ersatz," Haley announced, "not real coffee, and the bread has sawdust in it." I assumed he was joking about the bread, but after a few bites decided that maybe he wasn't.

When we were through eating I told them I needed to rest. "Don't use the mattresses," Corrigan warned, referring to a pile of straw-filled burlap sacks.

"Why not?"

"They have bugs in them."

Undeterred, I put one on a cot, another on top of me for warmth, and for the first time in weeks slept through the night. The next morning red spots that itched like the dickens covered my skin from head to foot. I searched for the culprits but detected nothing, and from then on had no mattress under or over me. The spots and itching disappeared in a couple of days.

Visiting with the others, and listening to their conversations, I found out more about them. Dillon's wife was seven months pregnant; he feared that a "missing" telegram might cause her to miscarry. Borg assured him the baby would live and be all right even if it arrived early. Placek described his captain as a "no-good loudmouth" who sneaked away during difficult battles. Corrigan's C.O. died trying to rescue a machine gunner pinned down by enemy fire. O'Connor's platoon was "annihilated." Replacements were provided; before he determined their capabilities or even learned their names, half of them were casualties. He was given command of a company which had lost all its officers the previous day. Platoon leaders from a reserve division reported to him. "Nobody knew who was who. Some lieutenant talked to me for ten minutes before realizing he was in the wrong battalion." Borg and his runner were taken prisoner while checking a supposedly unoccupied area. When the two from the Air Corps discussed clubs they went to in England and France between missions, I thought of infantrymen in muddy foxholes, but hearing how Minter was struck in the face by flak and bullets tore open Haley's legs made it clear that they too had suffered.

I mentioned the disgraced feeling being captured gave rise to. "That's ridiculous," Placek replied. "There's no disgrace unless you were a coward." I didn't think I'd been a coward but was aware of things I could have done differently, like looking behind me oftener or, better yet, not dropping off Sabatini and Polk; surely one of them would have seen those Krauts approaching. I should have crawled faster toward the outpost instead of letting myself be slowed down by excessive caution or fear. That my role as a combat lieutenant had ended in this manner seemed sad.

Time passed slowly. We were cold as well as hungry. The bread I saved for the next day's breakfast failed to satisfy my craving for food, and from mid-morning on I sweated out arrival of our rations at three.

Wandering through the building one afternoon I tested the front door to see if it was locked. It was. In an empty room I discovered a tube of antiseptic ointment and applied a little to my shrapnel wound, which hadn't healed and appeared to be infected. To relieve my boredom I drew floor plans for houses on sheets of paper that were lying around.

The German corporal who brought our food pulled me aside and castigated the Jews. "Would you allow your daughter to marry one?" he asked. "What difference does it make?" I thought, but said nothing. I'd heard about Hitler's anti-Semitism but didn't realize that Jews were being murdered or worked to death in concentration camps.

"Why is the U.S. fighting here instead of using its money to eliminate slums? There are no slums in Germany."

"We're fighting here to keep you from oppressing other countries," I answered. He laughed. "Germany is only seeking its own nationals. Germany needs living space. Germany is crowded. Why should the United States have all that space when we have none?" His voice seemed a bit hysterical.

"How much do you want?" I commented sarcastically, thinking of the countries they'd invaded. He took it as a question. "Alsace-Lorraine and part of Poland. Letting them be free is the same as Kentucky seceding in the American Civil War."

"How do we know you'll stop there? We can't believe Hitler."

"And we can't believe the U.S. because of Wilson."

When I referred to the bombing of London he responded that the English started it by dropping incendiaries on Berlin. He talked about the many years required for Germany to become a nation and how awful it would be if she were partitioned.

Several of his statements made no sense, but I was impressed by his wealth of information and ability to express himself. Dillon told me he'd received special training in order to influence American prisoners.

The bridge over the Rhine and a row of barrage balloons protecting it were clearly visible from our windows. A shelter in the basement was available if bombers showed up. One night they did. Awakened by yells from the others and the commotion of their dash for the stairs, I debated whether to join them. When explosions began shaking the walls and plaster fell from the ceiling, I hastened below.

The next morning guards announced that we were leaving. I stuck my house plans, ointment and remaining bread in a pocket. They marched us along the streets of Strasbourg. Pedestrians glared; a few hissed or shouted remarks that sounded nasty. Someone threw a rock; it landed harmlessly on the pavement. At the railway station a large number of P.O.W.'s — officers and enlisted men from various countries — had been assembled. Each of us was given a loaf of bread, then put in a boxcar. There were about 40 in mine; we sat on the floor, arms wrapped around our knees, crowded but not jammed together like sardines. Two circular openings the size of dinner plates provided ventilation and light.

Progress was slow. We waited on side tracks for hours. Once in awhile we were allowed to get out. On one of those occasions the guards handed me a container of marmalade and said to see that every prisoner received half a teaspoonful. Some of them had already eaten their entire loaf of bread; but most, not knowing how long the trip would last or if more would be issued, attempted to conserve. We also got, during that stop, two boiled potatoes apiece. No other food was furnished and no water. By the end of the third day, nobody had anything left.

Hungry and thirsty, we discussed the length of time a person could stay alive without nourishment. Did death from starvation precede death from dehydration, or was the opposite true? We also discussed when our train would reach wherever it was going, what might happen then, and whether any protection was available if Allied planes strafed or bombed us. Conversation diminished as discomfort grew.

Groups arranged themselves so that each man's pulled-up legs served as a backrest for the person in front of him. If several stood, those who were sitting could change positions and slide around a little. At night we lay on our sides, facing the same way, so everybody could stretch out. This also helped us keep warm, but almost any movement disrupted whoever was next to you. Much shifting and squirming occurred, making sleep difficult.

On the fifth day, from a siding near Limburg, in Germany, we were marched to a P.O.W. transit camp, lined up, and again searched. A guard seized my house plans and gave them to a young officer; together they turned the sheets back and forth, up, down, diagonally and sideways, trying to figure out what the drawings revealed. I couldn't avoid laughing – inwardly, of course — at their perplexed expressions.

A different guard examined the YD shoulder patch on my field jacket. I noticed him with a German non-com a moment later, pointing in my direction. The NCO started toward me, opening his pocket knife as he approached. What's he going to do, I wondered; stab my arm to see if I flinch or cry out? Are prisoners tormented or sadistically "tested" in this manner? The blade wasn't big enough to cause serious injury, but it could hurt. I grit my teeth. He took ahold of the patch, cut the threads, jerked it off, and walked away. His child must be collecting them, or he himself is, I surmised, breathing a sigh of relief. Now they would have another one.

My relief was short-lived; he returned a minute or two later and guided me into a building where a German major asked when I came overseas. I told him that only my name, rank and serial number could be disclosed. Though not scared, I was concerned; if no other YD officers had been captured, I might be important to him. "If you do not answer," he replied, "you will be sent to a worse place and lose time or maybe your mind" – at least that's how it sounded; his English was a little hard to understand. When I remained silent he nodded to the guard and we went back outside. My Strasbourg buddies thought his reference to a worse place was a bluff.

An "Oberleutnant" announced that all prisoners must be

deloused. I didn't know whether delousing involved the person or what he was wearing or both. Someone mentioned that people in concentration camps were put to death by having them strip for showers, then leading the group into a gas chamber. "P.O.W.'s aren't executed," I observed, but the possibility that this might happen lingered as we removed our clothes in a decrepit structure, dropped them on the floor and were herded into a room that had rows of pipes with shower heads – or were they gas jets? – criss-crossing the ceiling. Pieces of soap were on a table beside the door. Soap wouldn't be furnished, I reasoned, if this was a gas chamber. Unless it had been placed there to fool us.

The jets hissed and ice-cold water shot forth. I bathed quickly, hurried to my clothes, put them on, then raced to a wagon from which loaves of bread were being distributed. They ran out, but a Russian officer with two gave me one of his. We were told to "share"; reluctantly I broke mine apart and was handing half of it to an artilleryman when a German corporal called my name and four others. The five of us – a master sergeant, a staff sergeant, two privates and myself – he stated, would spend the night at Diez, a nearby town, and come back in a day or two. We got soup and hot coffee before leaving; it tasted good but didn't eliminate my gnawing hunger.

I visited with Master Sergeant Gunther as we walked along a dusty road. The German major, he said, warned him that P.O.W.'s who refused to answer questions were turned over to the Gestapo, but a Kraut non-com acknowledged that this rarely happened.

When we rounded a curve, half an hour later, I saw ahead of us a medieval castle similar to those pictured in children's fairy tale books. It was several stories high, built of stone, and had a slate roof from which dormers projected. A square tower with turrets at each corner was silhouetted against the setting sun. There were slits in the walls for defenders to fire through, and some windows had bars. Could this be our destination?

We reached it shortly after that, passed under an archway and crossed a courtyard to the far end of the castle. Stone steps, concave from centuries of use, rose up to an entrance. I looked at the menacing structure that loomed above me and had an empty feeling in the pit of my stomach.

We waited in a central hall while our guards obtained instructions, then went to an upper level where a dimly lit corridor extended into the distance. Metal doors lined both sides of it, each of them solid except for a small hole covered by a disc which could be pushed away to peek in. I knew instinctively that behind those doors were cells, probably for solitary confinement. This must be the worse place the major had referred to. Recalling Gunther's remark, I wondered if the Gestapo was in charge.

An old man in a threadbare uniform took me to one of the cells. The fading light of dusk coming through its window revealed a room approximately six feet wide and twelve feet long with partially plastered stone walls. Its only furnishings were a small four-legged stool, a straw-filled burlap mattress on a wooden frame, and a tin can that I concluded was the toilet. I hid a hunk of my bread in the mattress for consumption if they planned to starve me, and put the rest in my pocket so I'd have some if we left unexpectedly.

Pretty soon a guard unlocked the door and led me to where a German NCO in his early 20's, seated at a table, said, "Are you Lt. William D. Stevens?" I answered yes and commented on how American his English sounded.

"I grew up in Washington, D.C.," he replied. "My father served in our Diplomatic Corps."

He offered me coffee, which I accepted and drank while he studied a file. When the cup was empty, he refilled it. Surely, I thought, this soldier who was raised in the United States and talks like we do and understands our customs could not be part of Hitler's dreaded Gestapo.

"Is there anything you need?" he inquired, glancing up from the papers in front of him. I mentioned food and blankets. The kitchen, he explained, was closed, but perhaps a blanket could be obtained.

His congeniality and concern encouraged me to ask the question foremost in my mind: "Why am I here?"

The response took me by surprise: "Because you're suspected of being a spy. You may be shot tomorrow." I looked for a smile, assuming this was American-style kidding, but none appeared. He pushed my folder aside, picked up another file, and had a guard return me to my cell.

I sat on the edge of the bunk, confused and perplexed. The statement about shooting me couldn't be true; P.O.W.'s weren't shot. And yet that's what he'd said. Did the fact that I was caught behind their outpost make a difference; did they suspect that I let myself be captured in order to check on them and report back in some clandestine manner? I slid across the burlap mattress, leaned against the wall, pulled my legs up, wrapped my arms around them, and considered what might happen next. That they would shoot me was inconceivable; I simply didn't believe it. He must have been joking. Maybe I misunderstood. They might, however, employ third-degree tactics, or beat me, or provide only minimal food and water. By persevering I would prove to them, and to myself, that I was a good soldier.

All of a sudden I seemed to be staring down a long, pipe-like tunnel eight or ten feet in diameter. I could see daylight at the far end but not what lay beyond. That changed and I was gazing out of it at events from earlier years. My life didn't pass in review; I simply caught glimpses of certain people and occasions. Reality returned in less than 30 seconds and I found myself thinking about how a person ought to live. Is being conscientious and trying to do what's right important? My high school pal Chip Baker, who rarely studied and was often in trouble, appeared to have more fun than anybody else. Had I, by following the rules, missed the boat? No; not doing what I felt was right would have resulted in misery, not happiness.

Sleep eventually came. I dreamed I was standing in front of a firing squad, waiting for bullets to enter my body. Nothing happened and the scene faded away. When my eyes opened it was light outside.

My window – the double-hung type with several panes of glass in each half – had no bars. I raised the bottom section, leaned across the sill, and examined the ground 60 feet below me. It was too far to jump even if I landed on one of the shrubs or small trees growing among the rocks. There weren't any ledges or indentations in the wall to hang from or use as toeholds. Since I was no longer in the midst of enemy troops, escape might be possible. Would I be able to hide in barns or haystacks during the day and travel by night to Allied territory? How far would I have to go? In what direction? Would sympathetic families furnish food and help me?

The castle overlooked Diez. Shops with living quarters above them surrounded the town square; a river meandered nearby; railroad tracks curved into the hills beyond. Children were playing in grassy areas. A few women and two or three elderly men were on the sidewalks. Goose-down quilts aired on the sills of apartment windows; inside, housewives bustled about. A woman carrying an unwrapped loaf of bread emerged from a bakery. A sign on another building said Erich Kunkel. Everything seemed peaceful.

The skin had pulled apart in the middle of my leg wound, leaving a raw spot on which there was no scab. I applied more ointment and began reading a pocket-sized copy of St. Matthew given to me by the chaplain at Fort Jackson. Once in awhile I heard voices in the hall. Except for that and the occasional opening or closing of a door, silence reigned.

In the middle of the afternoon I was taken to an office on the main floor. A German captain, pointing to the chair in front of his desk, said in a friendly voice, "Sit down, Lt. Stevens." I couldn't have looked like much of an officer to him – unshaven, my formerly close-cropped hair shaggy and matted, my clothes disheveled and dirty – but I was determined to act like one and reveal nothing but my name, rank and serial number.

He offered me a cup of coffee, which I accepted, and an American cigarette, which I refused; then casually remarked, "So you're from Lincoln, Nebraska. Tell me, did they ever pave the road to Columbus?"

My jaw dropped. I'd traveled that road in college with a law school buddy who frequently mentioned the Highway Department's plan to hard-surface it. "You mean Columbus, Nebraska?" I responded in amazement.

"Yes. A lot of folks were pushing for pavement because the gravel created so much dust."

"But how would you know that?"

"I worked in a filling station there before the war."

"No, they didn't," I replied rather lamely, uncertain whether or not to believe him.

He talked about farming and his employment in various sections of the United States. It finally occurred to me that we were chatting away like old pals when all I'd intended to disclose was my name, rank and serial number. He smoked leisurely and sipped his coffee from time to time — hoping, no doubt, that I too would be relaxed.

"What company were you with?" he asked, removing my YD patch from an envelope.

"I can give only my name, rank and serial number."

He put a mark in his notebook, and after refilling my cup asked other questions. They seemed unimportant but I didn't answer them.

"Why am I here?"

"To check your identity. We have to confirm that you're a soldier, not a spy." Until then, he stated, I would receive soup, bread and coffee and could use the latrine if accompanied by a guard.

Back in my room I felt as if a weight had been lifted from my shoulders. There would be no third-degree after all, no starvation, no abuse, no firing squad. The man in the threadbare uniform showed up with two blankets, a cup, bowl and spoon. Growing hungrier by the minute, I sat on the four-legged stool waiting for chow. It arrived at 4. The soup was watery but palatable; the coffee, ersatz; the bread, coarse but free of sawdust. I ate slowly, savoring every bite, then arranged the blankets on my bed, crawled between them, thanked God for preserving me, prayed for strength to endure whatever I might have to face, and fell asleep.

The next morning a guard brought coffee and a spoonful of jam, which I spread on the bread from Limburg. After finishing it I watched the townspeople from my window and read more of St. Matthew.

The guy from Columbus sent for me about noon. He wanted to know when I came overseas. I refused to say.

"When did you join YD?"

"In December," I responded, figuring this wouldn't help him any. He asked which army corps my division was assigned to and what divisions were in that corps. I shook my head and kept quiet.

"If you're a soldier you'll be given Red Cross food and go to an officers camp in Poland until the war ends; if you're a spy the treatment is different. These inquiries are not interrogation, they're for identification," he declared, irritated, apparently, by my failure to speak.

"Your men know I'm a soldier. They captured me at the front. I'm obeying orders in refusing to answer, just as you would do if things were the other way around."

"I believe you," he replied, "but my chief isn't satisfied. It's not fair for your country to drop spies behind our lines. If these questions aren't answered you will be transferred to a worse place." Though discouraged by this second reference to a worse place, I remained silent.

"Well, think it over; we'll talk again tomorrow morning," he said, and as I was leaving called out, "I'll be seeing you." That reassured me; it sounded so American, so like a friend.

In my cell I realized that his statements about proving I wasn't a spy were malarkey. A spy would be briefed in advance and have better information than a soldier. I renewed my determination to be firm and tell him nothing when I returned the following day.

Nobody came for me the following day. Another passed, and then another, without any word. Has he forgotten, or been replaced, or become involved in an emergency? That he might intentionally be delaying didn't occur to me.

Conversing with the person who delivered the soup proved to be impossible. He looked tired, acted grumpy, and if he understood English pretended not to. So did my guards, who responded with uncomprehending stares to anything I said or growled sentences that conveyed no meaning. I decided to break the monotony by having them escort me to the latrine. Making my wishes known took a number of imaginative gestures – they'd have won first prize in a game of Charades – and when we got there I wished I hadn't bothered. The room was dirty and smelly, contained only a big barrel with a wooden plank across the top, and had neither toilet paper nor any substitute. From then on I used my tin can, emptying it out the window when necessary.

One night I dreamed that Dad had died. I attempted, upon awaking, to recall the details. His body was propped up in a bed. Friends were standing beside it consoling Mother. Although I didn't believe dreams revealed what was happening elsewhere or going to happen in the future, one couldn't be sure. Had worrying about me caused his death? This mustn't be allowed to prey on my mind, I concluded; dreams are figments of the imagination, not reality. But I couldn't keep from wondering, when I asked God to be with my family during the uncertainty they were now or soon would be facing: "Is he or is he not alive?"

Watching housewives and children lost its appeal and I found myself looking at the hills. Why are we fighting these people? Civilized human beings should be able to settle their differences without war. I thought about the future, recalling the vision of myself with a wife and children, practicing law in Lincoln, or pictured in minute detail the lavish meals I would have in New York City before returning home and the civilian clothes I would buy. A couple of times I remembered my first night in the castle. Why had I seemed to be gazing down a long tunnel? Why did events from the past spontaneously appear? Why did I recall Chip Baker and ponder whether I had "missed out" by obeying the rules? Why, in a dream, did I see myself in front of a firing squad? Was I subconsciously anticipating death?

Four days after my interrogator said we would talk again "tomorrow," he called me back and, pointing to a slip that had "Inf AA 80 Bn" written on it, inquired, "What does this mean?" I knew but didn't speak. "Where is the U.S. Fourth Army?" Annoyed by my silence, he remarked rather testily, "I'm trying to help but you won't cooperate. Let me show you something." He walked across the room and pulled open a closet door. I half expected to see a skeleton hanging there with a noose around its neck, or medieval torture instruments. Instead, stacked from floor to ceiling were cartons that had "American Red Cross Prisoner of War Food Parcel" printed on them. He picked up one, carried it to his desk, and held it so I could look inside. A package of Kraft cheese was near the top; next to it a box of Sunmaid raisins, packs of cigarettes, and a D-bar. My mouth watered but I didn't say anything.

"This is what you'll get if you answer our questions." I shook my head. He shrugged, closed the carton, and put it away. I wasn't aware that parcels like this existed. Food; real food; American food!

"What are the questions?"

"There are four of them: which regiments are in the 26th Division, what corps the division is attached to, the other divisions in that corps, and where the U.S. Fourth Army is."

"You know I can't tell you that."

We visited on subjects unrelated to war. Eventually he signalled for the guard, and when I stood up to leave said, as he had the previous time, "Well, think about it." Back in my cell I did think about it, and in the days that followed continued to think about it – a lot!

Every so often, in addition to soup and bread, I received boiled potatoes. One meal included a dab of cottage cheese; another, a thin slice of processed meat similar to Spam. Once they gave me a piece of corned beef that had greenish mold on it. I ate the untainted part and considered whether to avoid the risk of food poisoning by discarding the rest. I couldn't; my hunger was too great. Having learned in Boy Scouts that if you eat something and it isn't okay your stomach will growl, I bit off a sliver, chewed carefully, waited for what seemed like 30 minutes but was probably just two or three, and hearing no growls consumed it all – with no ill effects.

I drew house plans on the wall and endeavored to create a crossword puzzle (not having an eraser made both projects difficult), began memorizing the Sermon on the Mount, and spent much of one day making a deck of cards out of the little box my tube of ointment came in. After laboriously drawing 52 rectangles approximately three-eighths of an inch wide and half an inch long, I separated them by folding the pasteboard from side to side, marked each to indicate the card it represented, and played a game of Solitaire. They were too small to handle easily, and bending over while sitting cross-legged on the floor was uncomfortable, so I quickly lost interest.

Dusk was nostalgia time. What are the folks and David doing? I remembered our family card games and, with poignant longing, our meals together. Every Saturday during the depression years a client of Dad's who couldn't pay his bill brought us a chicken, which Mother baked or fried for Sunday noon dinner. Monday evenings we had chicken stew; Tuesday evenings, chicken soup. Mike and I "clucked" and claimed we would soon be laying eggs. Gee, if only I had a chicken now! I'd eat it raw – including the feathers!

Memories came of ROTC, OCS, Camp Campbell, maneuvers, and Fort Jackson; of Sabatini, Polk, Mahlin and Kaz. Would it matter to them, or anyone else, if I disclosed which three infantry regiments were in our division? What difference could that possibly make to the soldiers still there? Answering the next two questions was impossible because I didn't know which corps YD was in or what divisions the corps included. I did, however, know the whereabouts of the Fourth Army. A friend of mine who was assigned to one of its units had written me in July that they were at Fort Sam Houston, Texas. This, I realized, might be valuable to German intelligence and shouldn't be revealed. I could lie and say I hadn't the slightest idea where our Fourth Army was. Day after day, sitting on my bunk, my stool or the floor, and lying in bed at night, I debated whether telling my interrogator what regiments were in the division would adversely affect anybody. Was this a scrap of information which, fitted together with others, would provide the picture our enemy needed, or did it have no significance at all? Why not rejoin the group at Limburg? Aren't I being bull-headed – foolish? No, I decided; maybe it's the scrap they require. Also, you're not supposed to tell. Don't forget duty and honor. Be strong.

Eventually I was taken back to him. We talked about Nebraska and were discussing major league baseball when he said,

"Let's get this over with, Stevens. All you have to do is answer my questions."

"What if I don't know the answers?"

"You know which infantry regiments are in this division," he asserted, holding up my YD patch. "Answer what you can." I was tempted, but remained silent. "All right," he exclaimed, and banging his fist on the desk summoned the guard. I suspected on the way to my cell that the worse place lay not far ahead.

The hours went by more slowly than ever. Looking out the window no longer interested me, nor did reading St. Matthew. I tapped on the wall and called through the peep hole in my door, hoping for a response, but got none, then walked back and forth for exercise and to keep from becoming despondent. One afternoon the whine of air raid sirens caused a few mothers to round up their children; everybody else seemed unconcerned. No planes appeared. On another occasion the sirens sounded at night. Each morning I drew a line on the wall and wondered when, if ever, my interrogator would release me.

Could it be, I asked myself, that the answers to his questions actually are for identification? After all, I was captured in territory held by German troops. Maybe his chief really does think I'm a spy. YD's principal units must be known to him; the first words spoken to me in that underground bunker were, "You are from the one-o-four regiment?" The 26th Division sergeant I saw at Saverne said his captors knew which regiment he came from. Weren't the Krauts entitled to have their questions answered; wasn't I, having been caught by them, obligated to answer even though the instructions from our army were to disclose nothing but my name, rank and serial number? I didn't realize that under the terms of the Geneva Convention the Krauts had no right to such information and I had no duty to furnish it.

If only there were somebody to talk to. Even if he was as uncertain as I, we could encourage each other, lend one another support.

Once in awhile I talked to myself. "Go ahead and tell. Who cares? Staying here is stupid."

"No, Steve, that's not true. Don't give up. You've been in tough spots before."

"Not tough ones like this."

"Hold out. You can do it."

"I'll try."

Every night I resolved to hold out "one more day."

When my pal from Columbus finally had me brought back, his earlier friendliness returned. After pouring a cup of coffee for each of us, he asked if I was ready to answer the four questions. I replied no.

"Lieutenant, who do you think is going to win this war?"

There wasn't any doubt in my mind about that. We were. Should I say so or not?

He said it for me. "You are, you and your allies. Germany will be defeated. It's only a matter of time. Isn't it foolish to be shot as a spy when you can relax in a P.O.W. camp until the war ends?"

That hit home. Although I had never believed they would shoot me, and still didn't, why remain in solitary confinement, or be moved to a worse place, when our forces were winning and soon would prevail. Sensing, perhaps, a weakening of my resolve, he went to the closet for a Red Cross food parcel and laid it on his desk. I stared at that unopened box for what seemed like hours, fighting temptation, then blurted out: "YD's infantry regiments are the 101st, 104th and 328th. I don't know what corps we're a part of, what other divisions are in it, or where the U. S. Fourth Army is." He wrote something on a sheet of paper, pushed the carton my way, and pressed his buzzer. Neither of us spoke. When the guard entered I stuck the parcel under my arm and followed him to my cell.

Elation should have enveloped me: the longed-for prize at last was mine, my ordeal would now be over. Instead, I felt like a traitor, sick at heart as if I had sold my birthright for a mess of pottage. I pulled the flaps apart slowly, almost reluctantly, as though I had no right to this treasure, and carefully examined the contents: vitamin pills, crackers, peanut butter, jelly, oleo, Spam, canned salmon, powdered milk and coffee, in addition to what I'd seen in the previous one. Unwrapping the cheese, I broke off some and ate it with a cracker. This parcel contained prunes rather than raisins; I had two of them, and a little chocolate for dessert. Slipping a pack of cigarettes into my pocket to use as a medium of exchange, I sat on the floor, dejected and ashamed.

Several hours later a different guard appeared. I picked up the carton, expecting to depart. He made me put it down. "Oh no, surely they won't make me leave this. Dear Lord, please don't let them. I'm so hungry, so terribly hungry." It finally became clear that we would be returning.

I was led to the interrogator's office. "Have a seat," he said. "My major isn't satisfied with your information. I'll have to ask you additional questions."

Infuriated, I jumped up from my chair, snapped, "Your major can go to hell; I'm not telling you or him or anyone else a goddam thing," and walked over to the door, intending to yank it open and put my fist in the face of whoever was standing there. I was mad — mad at him, mad at myself, mad at the whole rotten, stinking world — and sick enough of all this crap that I didn't care what happened. Never, ever would I say another word to these sons of bitches. If they sent me to a worse place, so be it.

"Very well, Lieutenant," he responded quietly. "Good luck." I hadn't anticipated that and, taken by surprise, looked back at him, sitting behind his desk lighting a cigarette. A guard came in and motioned to me. I looked again at this man who claimed to have lived in Nebraska, uncertain whether to say goodbye, thank you, or nothing at all. He had turned away and was dialing somebody on the telephone — his major, no doubt, or maybe his mistress. I never saw him again.

After getting my food parcel, jacket and mess gear, I went to a room that had a table and chairs in the middle of it, ceiling lights, and four double-decker bunks. I ate a small amount of salmon from my Red Cross box, thumbed through a book entitled *The Dark Forest*, then, emotionally drained, rolled into one of the beds. Pencilled on a wall beside it was the phrase, "Ne illegitimi tu carborundum," or something like that, presumably Latin for, "Don't let the bastards wear you down." A coat-of-arms with a chamber pot as the central feature had been drawn above it, and underneath were half a dozen names, including that of Kevin Hawthorne, a fellow I'd known at the university. I wanted to mull over the day's events, but drifted off instead.

Two guards came for me in the morning. The castle, as we left, appeared even more menacing than it had the evening of my arrival. "What next?" I wondered.

7

The building in Limburg that housed captured officers was filled with triple-tiered bunks and smoke. Half a dozen Americans – resting, cooking, eating, talking – occupied the "cubicle" I was led to. They greeted me and a captain demonstrated how to cut German bread into thin slices and toast them on a stove made from the tin cans in Red Cross parcels. Heat was produced by burning part of the carton or wood shavings whittled from a bed slat. The stoves, created by English P.O.W.'s, were called Smokey Joes. The name seemed appropriate.

Borrowing the captain's knife, I carefully severed three pieces from my cheese and one from my bread for an open-faced sandwich, which I toasted and ate with the soup our captors brought. What a treat! And how marvelous to be among friends!

That afternoon each of us got three small potatoes, boiled in their skins. I watched a lieutenant dice his, cut up some Spam, mix them together, add margarine and salt, heat the concoction, and have hash for dinner. When an opportunity came to use the stove, I did this too. It tasted great but failed to satisfy my craving for food.

The barracks was cold so we burned a bed slat (secretly, this being *verboten*) in one of the ceramic tile heaters that were supposed to provide warmth.

The following day guards loaded us into boxcars for the trip to Oflag 64, near Schubin, in Poland. Mine was so crowded we couldn't all sit at the same time and had to take turns standing. Lying down was impossible. Our drawn-up knees, when we sat, were spread apart so the man ahead would fit between them; there wasn't room enough to make a back rest for him by keeping them together. Extending a leg to relieve cramped muscles and aid circulation disrupted everybody near you. We slept slumped forward or leaning against an adjacent shoulder, but later developed a rotation system where more stood so that nine or ten could stretch out for awhile.

The train stopped frequently and every so often we were allowed to get off and walk around. This enabled me to locate a guard who would exchange part of his bread ration for cigarettes. Twice we received soup; it was awful but helped fill our stomachs.

By the end of the second day many in my boxcar had no Red Cross food left. I anguished over whether it was selfish not to share with them what remained of mine, or foolish to when none of us knew how long the trip would last. Should those who conserved assist those who didn't? I gave a few guys cigarettes to smoke or use for trading, and occasionally a prune or bit of cheese. As the contents of my parcel dwindled, this became increasingly difficult to do and I began eating at night so the ones with nothing wouldn't see me. By the fifth day all of it was gone.

To keep our spirits up we told jokes, described combat experiences, and discussed post-war plans. Now and then somebody whistled or hummed a tune. There were periods of quiet, too, when we sat in silence, each wrapped in his own thoughts, yearning for this agony to end.

Despite our discomfort, no one got nasty or went berserk. What bothered me most was being so cramped, unable to move my legs, bend over, stretch, or change positions. I looked forward to standing, but tired of it quickly and was anxious to sit again. The odor of urine and fecal matter fouled the air. At times the torment was so intense I felt I could no longer endure it. Each day seemed an eternity. Never in my life had I been so miserable.

The only good thing was that, unlike solitary confinement, I didn't have to go through this by myself; others were with me. Once, a guy sang, very softly, "When you're down and out, lift up your head and shout, there's gonna be a great day." That helped us all. It was a needed admonition not to despair, a subtle reminder that better things were coming.

Twice, due to expected strafing attacks, we had to lie down on the roadbed. Whether this was for our safety or the train crew's wasn't revealed.

The morning of the eighth day, we left the boxcars and marched to Oflag 64. A high, barbed-wire fence with guard towers surrounded it. Ten or fifteen feet inside that fence was another one; inside it were a number of buildings, two of them rather imposing. After receiving a hot meal, we met with Lt. Col. Grabau in the brick barracks our group would occupy. Colonel Goode, he said, as S.A.O. (Senior American Officer) in this camp, was in charge of all P.O.W.'s – subject, of course, to limitations imposed by the Germans. We were to obey his orders, maintain a soldierly bearing and appearance, shave regularly, and stay physically fit by walking along a path near the fences. Under no circumstances should we attempt to get away; all escape plans must be submitted to and approved by the S.A.O. The Krauts required us to gather twice a day for "appel," a formation that permitted them to determine whether everybody was present or accounted for. Hot coffee would be provided in the morning, soup and bread at noon, and something for supper. Each of us would be given a Red Cross parcel but it might be awhile before more could be issued. Medical care was available for those who needed it.

I didn't, thank heavens; our train trip hadn't caused any health problems and the sore on my leg appeared to be healing. To me, a place like this seemed wonderful. "It's a good camp," Grabau remarked.

Six of us used three double-deck bunks plus some wooden lockers to form a small "sub-cubicle," and scrounged from an unoccupied section of the building a table and four stools for it. We were pleased with the result.

Our first appel came at four that afternoon. P.O.W.'s streaming from various buildings lined up by platoons and stood at parade rest while guards shuffled by counting heads. A conference ensued in which Col. Goode and his staff participated.

Was a man missing or had they counted wrong? After appel, Austin (one of my cubicle mates) and I walked for exercise and agreed that we would do this daily.

That evening I eagerly consumed the boiled potatoes we got for supper instead of saving one, as experienced prisoners nearly always did, to snack on later or have for breakfast the next day. By 10 o'clock, when the lights went off, I was asleep.

The following morning we talked about stool pigeons. Had "fake" P.O.W.'s been scattered among us to see what was happening? My experience in the castle showed how fluent in English and familiar with our customs Germans who'd lived in America were. They would have plenty to report: a tunnel was being dug and clandestine radios picked up BBC news broadcasts. To minimize the risk of "stoolies," one or more old-timers interviewed every newcomer. I'd spoken briefly to Kevin Hawthorne and expected him to vouch for me.

It turned out that somebody else did: Art Sampson, a Lincolnite I knew slightly. "Fancy meeting Bill Stevens here," he said, strolling into our cubicle after appel. We visited and I eagerly absorbed what he told me about Oflag 64. Originally a school for Polish boys, it was converted to a "lager" for American ground force officers captured by Rommel's tank units in North Africa. Swedish YMCA representatives had brought in books, sports equipment and musical instruments. Classes taught by P.O.W.'s with training or experience in a particular subject were held regularly; there was a law course I could attend. A band had been organized. Vocal and dramatic groups presented programs from time to time. Volunteers manned a library in the main building. Art's room mate, Joe Keller, was in charge of it; perhaps he would let me assist there, this being "the only warm place in camp." Those who listened to the illicit radios, which had been constructed with materials hidden in parcels from home, obtained by bribing guards, stolen from an old public address system, and pilfered from various sources, communicated to their buddies anything of importance. They passed it on to all who could be trusted.

He explained the P.O.W. vocabulary to me. We were kriegies, from the German word Kriegsgefangener, which meant prisoner of war. The guards were called goons. Hearing what BBC reported was "listening to the bird." Our ersatz coffee was referred to simply as "ersatz"; the water they gave us as "heise" – Deutsch for hot. Red Cross parcels were "Number 10's." A bash was any concoction created by a kriegie from the food in his Number 10 or from that furnished by the goons. To bash was to eat the concoction.

Art believed my parents would be notified soon, if they hadn't already been, that I was at Oflag 64. He heard from his family regularly and would ask them in his next letter to telephone mine. Each kriegie was permitted to receive from home, once every two months, a package containing food, clothing, smoking materials, and articles for personal use. His most recent one included pajamas, which, since he already had a pair, he would bring to me.

That seemed like a nice gesture. I'd slept in my clothes since coming overseas; pajamas would make me feel more civilized. I hadn't brushed my teeth for weeks. My handkerchief was long gone. The winter underwear I'd worn since leaving Normandy was filthy and so were my sox; maybe they could be washed when we were allowed to take a shower. Fortunately my army boots were holding up well, not wearing out or pulling apart at the seams. I had no comb or brush for my hair, now a couple of inches long. Razors were available, so I was able to shave.

We got our Red Cross parcels later that day. Mine contained Klim, cheese, soluble coffee, sugar, oleomargarine, jam, chicken paté, Spam, crackers, prunes, a D-bar, five full-sized packs of cigarettes, seven vitamin pills, and two bars of soap. Some contained peanut butter. "Klim" was powdered milk.

So began my life at the permanent camp. Discomfort didn't disappear: it was cold in the barracks, gnawing hunger continued notwithstanding Red Cross and other food, and time still passed slowly. But things were much better than they had been. Surely the war would end soon.

Our ersatz coffee, delivered after morning appel, was hot; and though weak, provided needed liquid. Breakfast consisted of this plus items saved from the previous evening or taken from our No. 10's. I usually had a thin slice of bread with oleo and sugar on it, or a left-over boiled potato. Our noon soup was served in the mess hall, where we ate in shifts. American enlisted men helped prepare it; there were a number of them at Oflag 64 even though it had been established for officers. We also got one-sixth loaf of German bread. Sometimes the soup was good, sometimes not; if made from turnip greens or "grass" it was terrible. Now and then hunks of meat, fat or gristle could be seen. Once there was an eyeball floating in the kettle. Even I couldn't swallow that. Luckily, it drifted away as the server ladled out my portion.

Many of us saved part of our bread for "tea time" in the afternoon, when hot water, a cupful or more per man, was brought to the barracks. I put coffee in my "heise" and sipped it while eating pieces of bread (toasted on a Smokey Joe to lessen the sour taste) topped with jam, margarine or sugar – occasionally, flinging discretion to the winds, a little of each. Supper, in the mess hall, consisted of potatoes or boiled cabbage furnished by the goons, and canned salmon, Spam, Prem or bully beef taken from our Red Cross parcels before we received them.

We learned to be innovative with our food. Boiled spuds could be whipped, mashed, fried, kneaded into potato cakes by adding oleo and cracker crumbs, or used for hash. We cut dried bread crusts into tiny squares and called them Grape-Nuts. I stirred jam or pulverized prunes or chocolate scraped from a D-bar into a paste made from water, sugar and Klim, and consumed the result as if it were ice cream, prune whip, chocolate pudding or some equally exotic treat.

Letters home had to be on a form provided by the goons, which limited their length, and only one per week was allowed. My first, written shortly after we arrived, said, "Gosh how I hope you haven't worried about me. I am okay, not wounded, and in good health," then listed what they should send.

Somebody in our cubicle acquired a deck of cards. We used it a lot. I played Bridge, Poker, Hearts, and once in awhile Solitaire. We read, too, and talked, primarily about food, and most of the time were cheerful, not pessimistic, grumpy or down in the dumps. Every day Austin and I walked a mile or so outdoors.

A Belgian overcoat was issued to me when Sampson reported that I had nothing but a field jacket. It helped ward off the cold during appels; and, laid on top of my blankets, provided additional warmth at night. I also received a muffler, a cap, and a pair of gloves.

They were discussing contracts when I attended my first law class. Subsequent sessions dealt with criminal procedure, torts, evidence, and constitutional principles. I went regularly but didn't learn much – the room was chilly and my mind tended to wander. Joe Keller found a job for me in the library three evenings a week from 7 until 10 o'clock. The opportunity it provided to look for interesting books, and the fact that this really did appear to be "the only warm place in camp," made working there worthwhile.

My next letter to the family assured them that I wasn't being mistreated. "I hope you have mailed a box of food by now, and written." Not knowing how they were was a source of concern because of that dream about Dad.

Sampson obtained a composition book and pencil for me from a guard in exchange for cigarettes. I jotted down ideas my reading gave rise to and described in condensed form everything that happened between the division's departure from Normandy and my arrival at Schubin. I also used it as a diary:

> *Nov. 26: . . . Sunshine today and the Allies have Strasbourg except for the bridges. My food is getting short, but the war should be over by Dec. 15th.*

A kriegie who had two pipes let me have one of them. Puffing contentedly on tobacco from cigarettes, I thought about myself as a lawyer in Lincoln. There should always be candy bars in my desk drawer, I decided, and an ample supply of sweet rolls close by to snack on. Aware that the war against Japan must be won before this could occur, I acknowledged that civilian life might be "a long way off."

> *Nov. 29th: . . . Cold today – my feet bothered me, my throat is sore, and my nose is running most of the time. No classes tomorrow since it's Thanksgiving.*
>
> *Nov. 30th: . . . Lt. Blake preached a short "devotional" on what we have to be thankful for. I am thankful to be alive, for I realize so well how easily I could not be, and if still living, how I might be*

suffering from cold and damp and fatigue on the battlefronts. I will carry back with me a deep appreciation of food, shelter, safety and (because of my loneliness at Diez) companionship. Though I may have less this Thanksgiving for which to be thankful, never have I appreciated so truly and so deeply what I do have. . . .

Blake's devotional brought to mind the unsuspecting German soldier I shot on our combat patrol. Why did killing him cause no remorse, then or later? Because he was simply a silhouette moving through the dark? No, I'd have felt none even in broad daylight. We destroy the enemy, I concluded, so they won't destroy us. There's nothing personal about it. Even peace-loving people like me have no qualms about ending the lives of those we're fighting against. It's something you have to do. That's how wars are won.

Why, then, did I spare the guy who looked up with terror in his eyes? I had no answer to that. If he'd sneered, I would have killed him.

My thoughts turned to Thompson, the only First Platoon man who died while I was their leader. His death still saddened me. Was it he who wrote, on the *Saturnia,* "I know I will never see you again"? Did he have a wife? Children? Brothers, or was he his parents' only son? Did Kaz or Mahlin send a note to them? How many First Platoon soldiers have died by now? How many will die before the war is over?

My reading covered a wide range: American history, religion, law, mysteries, novels, poetry. "Francine," I observed in the composition book regarding *A Tree Grows In Brooklyn,* "perceives beauty and excitement everywhere, even at the public library. I must try to see the good in what's taking place and ignore the bad. I should eat more slowly, enjoy it more, pretend it's better than it really is."

On December 1st an American enlisted man cut my hair. I didn't ask whether he'd been a barber prior to entering the service, but was satisfied with the result and gave him five cigarettes.

Lt. Col. Grabau examined our bunks to find out how many slats each of them had. Additional ones were needed for the tunnel. Eyeing us for size, he determined who could or couldn't spare a few. Two of mine were removed; after rearranging those that remained, I carefully and with considerable trepidation crawled onto the bed. Would it hold me? It did; but at times the sound of a kriegie crashing to the bunk below him, or to the floor, reverberated through the building.

A committee supervised construction of the tunnel, assigning duties and hours to those who volunteered or were chosen to work on it. Some dug, lying on their backs or stomachs; others carried the excavated soil, hidden in Red Cross cartons or their clothes, to disposal areas. Sampson said the ceiling of one barracks sagged from the weight of dirt concealed above it. The entrance to the tunnel was underneath a floor; the exit would be outside the fences. Slats were used for shoring.

> *Dec. 2: Helped at the library awhile, had chow, and spent the afternoon reading, walking around, etc. The evening spent in the library. Gosh but I was cold today, especially my feet. A letter from Col. Goode to the Red Cross states that we are on a starvation diet, receiving less calories than a man in bed requires for sustenance. However, Number 10's are rumored close. Ate a little more from mine after our supper in the mess hall, but my hunger persists and I just try to take the edge off my appetite. Wrote the folks requesting a long list of food, then pictured in my mind the doughnuts, pie, ice cream, cake and chocolate malts I will feast on when I return. Wow!*

Would the colonel's letter accomplish anything? Was what it said true? I had read, once, about a man who starved to death. Could this be happening to us? My knowledge of calories, sustenance levels and the like was minimal. Did lack of food contribute to my constantly being so cold? I began sleeping in my clothes again to keep warm.

Hearing Beethoven's Symphony #5 at a recorded music program brought memories of OCS. Pete Shelton often played it on the Victrola in our day room. "What's happened to Tony and him?" I wondered. It's a good thing I didn't know. Both of them had soft jobs at bases in the U. S.

> *Dec. 6: . . . I got a Number 10 today but only nibbled into it, making two cheese sandwiches for "tea time" and adding sugar*

and milk to my coffee. I smoked my pipe and chatted with the others until appel. Suddenly I felt funny. Standing at appel I thought I might be sick to my stomach. After it was over I came in and stretched out on my bunk. . . . I suspected dysentery because it's so common and hard to avoid, but my condition seemed to be associated with weakness and lack of food. So I pulled out the new box and ate two crackers with oleo and strawberry jam, and three slices of bread with oleo and chicken paté. Ah, delicious, and right away I felt better. . . .

The P.O.W. band gave a concert. Hearing those songs from happier days was fun. I remembered dancing with Ginny at the Prom before she decided to marry Ken.

That night, lying in bed, I cursed myself for not asking her to marry me. Why did I think uncertainty about the future mattered? My life wasn't being disrupted more than anyone else's. We had so much in common and truly cared for each other. Our wedding could have been postponed until I received my commission. She'd have waited.

Every Saturday guards inspected our lockers to make sure we had no "contraband" and weren't hoarding edible items. Cans in our Red Cross parcels had to be opened immediately so their contents couldn't be saved for an escape.

Dec. 10: . . . I'm not having tea because after the noon soup I ate several pieces of toast with oleo and paté on them and two crackers with jam and drank a cup of hot chocolate. Someday that won't seem like much, but it's such a gigantic foray into my Red Cross box that it would be morally wrong (and not very smart) to eat more now. I dream of getting home so I can eat continuously.

On the 14th our clothes were deloused. While they went through a fumigation process, each krieigie had his weight checked. Mine, converted from kilograms, totaled 115. In two months I'd lost 50 pounds.

Returned from noon chow, having stowed away a good-sized bowl of soup, and proceeded to down two days bread ration, the rest of my strawberry jam and the rest of my grape jelly. In addition I made a cup of chocolate with half a square of D-bar and lots of sugar. But I'm not full. #10's are being issued and I'm supposed to get mine Monday. I have adequate cheese, prunes and oleo to last until then; also some paté-cheese mix and milk powder, and an extra half pound of cheese and an extra D-bar for which I owe the coffee from my next box. Then we get Christmas boxes, and starting Jan. 1st a parcel a week for awhile. So things look all right as far as the food situation is concerned . . .

"The war seems destined to go on until spring," December 18th's entry observes, "though I personally believe it will end this year. Most of the others, though, and especially the men who just arrived, say spring."

One of the new arrivals was a YD lieutenant named Seiboldt. He told me a few days later that everybody in the regiment assumed I'd been killed.

Officer casualties, he stated, have been close to 85%. This gave me something to think about. Where would I be if things hadn't turned out as they did? Dead? Or recovering in an English hospital from a million dollar wound? I don't know, but I recognized – as I have before since becoming a P.O.W. – that I am mighty lucky to be here, safe, secure, well, and spared from the suffering (to say the least) I surely would have experienced if it had been my lot to remain a platoon leader in Company E . . .

The division participated in two major battles during November, Seiboldt said, and lost a lot of men. He thinks a Silver Star was awarded to me for what I did before being captured. That probably isn't true, but how swell it would be if my contribution to the war effort was not "so little," as I have often felt.

Why, I asked myself, did I sully my record as a soldier by revealing which infantry regiments were in the 26th Division? What caused me to weaken? It was wrong to disclose this, wrong to conclude that enduring the uncertainty of solitary confinement was foolish. I realized almost immediately that I shouldn't have told him, and when called back said, "Your major can go to hell." If only I'd said that to him earlier. Filled with regret, I hoped my YD friends would never hear about this failure of fortitude and courage.

December 25th's entry describes Christmas eve as "different and sad." A kriegie choir sang carols. When they came to *Silent*

Night, I thought of my parents and brothers. Were they too singing, "Silent night, holy night, all is calm, all is bright"? Did they, like my comrades in the 101st, believe I was dead? Tears welled up in my eyes; I fought hard to hold them back. Soldiers don't cry.

Stomach cramps and diarrhea resulted in numerous trips to the latrine that night. The next day I "alternately felt better and worse." Our noon meal in the mess hall was fantastic but I ate very little of it. After sleeping "more than an hour," I joined Sampson and Keller in their building for Christmas dinner.

They had been planning it for weeks; including me was thoughtful and generous of them. We had turkey from our Red Cross parcels, gravy created out of chicken paté, boiled rice, date muffins (made from bread and cracker crumbs) topped with plum jam. Eating slowly in order to enjoy each bite and not overwhelm our stomachs, we talked, laughed and, after finishing the food, sipped tea for nearly an hour. The *pièce de résistance* followed: steamed pudding, with hard sauce prepared by Art and Joe using powdered milk, sugar, oleo and condiments from home. It was more than my ailing body could handle; I excused myself, hurried to the latrine, and threw up. "*C'est dommage*," the diary comments, but "we shared a swell meal."

On December 26th I read several chapters of *Jones On Evidence*, a law textbook, and a number of pages in *The Epic Of America*. The camp's supply of drinking water ran out, adding thirst to our woes. Standing on frozen ground twice daily for appel chilled our feet; the cold barracks chilled our bodies. I often went to bed early to keep warm. "I am hungry and thirsty and nostalgic and homesick," the concluding lines of my diary entry declare, but thankful "for the good things that are mine."

> *Sun., Dec. 31st. . . . What a strange, elusive, indescribable feeling I have as 1944 draws to a close. It has been the most eventful, far-reaching year of my life, and completely unlike previous ones. They were not always easy – I worked hard – but there was so much joy in them, so much happiness. That hasn't been true of this one; the pleasant times have been few and far between. From start to finish 1944 has been characterized by physical hardship and suffering. . . .*

May peace return to the world in 1945. . . . Until then, Heavenly Father, sustain me and bless my family and be with those who continue to fight and with all who suffer.

"We got No. 10's last Wednesday," I noted on Sunday, January 7th, "and it's been more or less a constant bash since." Blank pages remained in my composition book, but I didn't write in it again.

Despite the satisfactory situation with respect to food, our many books, the showers we were allowed to take now and then, the card games we played, and the companionship that existed, an undercurrent of unrest was developing – perhaps, ironically, because of the favorable war news. Germany's counteroffensive in the Ardennes had failed, Russia was advancing from the east, British and American bombers were wreaking havoc. Would these and other setbacks induce a defiant Hitler to retaliate against us? Hearing that his troops had massacred American P.O.W.'s at Malmedy caused us to feel less safe, less secure.

Icy winds whipped through our clothing at appels. The barracks seemed devoid of warmth. Our rations from the goons deteriorated in quality as well as quantity. The supply of No. 10's diminished to the point where two men had to share one instead of each receiving his own. Classes were discontinued because of waning interest due to lack of heat. I considered asking Kevin Hawthorne, who as a major was part of the S.A.O.'s staff, whether they had any plans. Was the tunnel going to be used? Grabau spoke to us once or twice but imparted little information.

One night the sound of a locker being opened awakened me. I ignored it and went back to sleep. The next morning a D-bar was missing from my Red Cross parcel. I was livid and wanted to tear the thief limb from limb but had no idea where to turn. Surely none of my cubicle mates – these guys with whom most of my waking hours were spent – would do this. Yet one of them must have.

I shaved regularly, sharpening the blade afterwards on a stone so it would be ready for another kriegie, drew sketches of a house I might someday have, participated in bull sessions and card games, read books (though less enthusiastically than before), and memorized Thomas Henley's *Invictus* because three of its verses appeared to be saying, like that motto on the castle wall, "Don't let the bastards wear you down."

Out of the night that covers me
Black as the pit from pole to pole
I thank whatever gods may be
For my unconquerable soul.

In the fell clutch of circumstance
I have not winced nor cried aloud
Under the bludgeonings of chance
My head is bloody but unbowed.

* * *

It matters not how strait the gate
How charged with punishment the scroll
I am the master of my fate
I am the captain of my soul.

"Am I the master of my fate?" I wondered. "Yes, if I keep a positive outlook, avoid self-pity, and don't let cold, hunger or discouragement get me down. I'll make it through this. I can do it. I'll be all right."

Our bird reported the names of Polish cities – places most of us knew nothing about – being abandoned as Russian troops advanced. On January 19th they reached Posnan. That name we recognized; Posnan wasn't far from Schubin. Germans who had settled in Poland after the Nazi occupation streamed along the road outside our fences, returning to their homeland. Far to the east we heard artillery shells exploding.

The announcement that Oflag 64 would be evacuated came the next day. We were to leave the following morning. Those too ill to go could stay behind. Why, I asked myself later, didn't they just let all of us stay? It would have been so much easier on everyone.

8

Anticipation and exhilaration abounded as we prepared for departure. Our Russian allies, drawing nearer all the time, would surely reach us soon. Until then, marching through rural Poland might be more exciting than sitting around waiting. On the other hand, Oflag 64 was a pleasant place to wait, so emotions were mixed. What little I had to take with me — a cup and spoon, an unopened package of cheese and two D-bars for emergency use, my pajamas, pipe and composition book — was in a rolled-up blanket that would be draped across one shoulder.

At the specified hour we grabbed our stuff and assembled for a final appel. It had snowed during the night, but there was no wind and the sun seemed about to break through the overcast. Confusion regarding the head count caused considerable delay. Goons scurried back and forth shouting orders; their officers conferred at length with ours. Finally we did a right face and, four-abreast, started toward the gate. Each kriegie, as he went by it, was given a Red Cross parcel. Before long, Oflag 64, which was to have been our permanent camp, disappeared from sight.

The column of fours became a column of threes or two's as we moved along the snow-covered road. No attempt was made to keep in step. Our guards being either old or lame, we walked slowly and stopped frequently. I ate some Prem and cheese from my new box and munched on the M & M's it contained. After awhile the road grew slippery. Every so often, artillery shells exploded behind us;

I looked back once and saw flashes along the horizon. According to our bird, Russian armies were less than 25 miles away.

Dusk descended but we kept going, eventually halting in a farmyard. My platoon was assigned to a large barn, dimly lit by kerosene lanterns inside the door. Austin, Potter and I found a spot near a tethered cow, spread out our blankets, and proceeded to bash, feeling that with liberation imminent we needn't conserve. I consumed all of my crackers, most of my pineapple jam, and half of my salmon. We took turns bringing hot water from the farmhouse and enjoyed "*beaucoups* coffee, sugar and milk." Fires were prohibited on account of the hay.

The three of us talked far into the night. Potter, who had decided to conceal himself and head east after everyone else left, wanted Austin and me to join him. "Austie" was all for it; I hesitated. Our instructions from the S.A.O. and his staff were to stay together because of the reprisals hiding or escaping might lead to for the rest of the group. The Ruski's, we'd been told, could repatriate a whole bunch of us more effectively than they could scattered groups of individuals. I thought about it a long time, weighing the pros and cons, before opting to remain. Why risk getting shot?

Excited voices awakened me at 3 a.m. The cow by us was giving birth. A farmer arrived, grabbed the calf's protruding legs, and pulled it out. Having never witnessed anything like this, I was fascinated. The calf, breathing heavily, lay still while its mother removed part of the placenta with her tongue. The farmer picked up his lantern and departed. Sitting in the darkness, I reflected on the incongruity of new life coming into existence while all around us war was bringing it to an end.

Some kriegies slipped away prior to daybreak. Others, including Potter and Austin, hid. Those physically unable to continue were not required to leave. The rest of us, a majority by far, formed platoons and moved on.

It was cold again, and additional snow had fallen, but the sun shone and walking helped keep us warm. Refugees by the thousands crowded the roads, pushing and pulling carts piled high with belongings, carrying babies and bags, going west, I assumed, to escape the hated Russians or the wrath of liberated Poles. Most of them were afoot; a few rode in wagons drawn by oxen or scrawny horses. I wondered if they had a destination and what would happen when they reached it. Sometimes I wondered that about us.

We crossed the Bromberg-Schneidernuhl Canal, which was guarded by a Kraut detachment, and late in the afternoon got to Eichfeld. We'd covered 45 kilometers, 21 the first day, 24 the second – roughly 27 miles. Rifle and machine gun fire in the distance indicated that the Ruski's were gaining on us. No food was provided. I ate Prem and cheese from my parcel and slept in a hay loft.

The long-awaited news came early the next morning: our guards had disappeared; we were free, liberated! Shouts of joy filled the air. Stay where you are, the S.A.O. said, pending further orders. We were given hot soup and a quarter-pound hunk of margarine. I finished my Prem and most of my box of raisins. The minutes ticked by. Was Colonel Goode with the Russians, arranging our transportation home? Joy changed to dismay when a German officer and Latvian SS personnel showed up. The Ruski's, according to a refugee, were at the canal we'd seen yesterday. One of their patrols had been ambushed; the bodies of those killed were on display in a nearby town for the locals to gawk at.

We left that afternoon for Charlottenburg, five kilometers away, traveling cross-country part of the time. Kraut soldiers manned machine guns along the road. Trucks loaded with German infantrymen dressed in white passed by. In Charlottenburg, while sleeping quarters were being commandeered, kriegies in the leading platoons traded cigarettes for bread and sausage; those of us farther back lost out. We were taken to a large shed, where I ate sparingly from my dwindling Red Cross supply. That night more of the group, disenchanted, hoping for something better, departed. I considered joining them but concluded that sticking together was smarter. Liberation must be close.

We received hot soup in the morning and resumed marching. When the column halted at Lobsens, a Polish woman standing by the street surreptitiously put an apple in my hand. I smiled and tried to give her cigarettes. She refused them. Surely these people don't have food to spare, I thought, touched by her generosity and the kind look on her face. We started forward, then stopped again. The proprietor of a nearby inn let me have a little cheese and ersatz coffee in exchange for cigarettes. I got a loaf of bread for a pack of Old Golds from someone in the doorway of a building. One of the SS men yelled at a housewife he noticed offering milk to a P.O.W., and drew his pistol.

My platoon was sent to a barn on the outskirts of town. A young girl filled my cup with water, which I heated over a fire in the yard. Three of us, pooling our blankets, slept together for warmth. The German commandant from Oflag 64, accompanied by the guards who departed two days earlier, returned. Our SS cadre, he announced, would fire into the hay to make sure nobody was hiding. When we were ready to leave, they did, while the rest of us watched. Several kriegies ran out; some remained. Cold and weary, we went 20 kilometers through a blizzard. That evening, sharing blankets with Shuster, I resisted the temptation to open my remaining Red Cross food – the package of cheese and two D-bars being saved for an emergency. The D-bars were in my pocket. I hid the cheese in a pile of straw by my head. The next morning it was gone. I dug in various places, thinking I might be mistaken about the spot, but in my heart knew that I wasn't. Some brother kriegie had seen me conceal it there and stolen it. Shuster? He seemed like too decent a guy. Frustrated, bitter and mad, I wondered how anyone could stoop so low.

Hot water was furnished and we were notified that this would be a day of rest. I gave a refugee family five cigarettes for a sandwich and stood in line quite awhile for "oatmeal soup." A dead Russian in the area that served as our latrine gazed with unseeing eyes at the sky. No indications of pain, agony, bliss or joy appeared on his silent face. "He's at peace now," I mused, staring at the lifeless body beside me.

We gulped down thin soup the following morning and journeyed on. Snow had fallen; our boots sank into it, inhibiting progress and consuming energy. Refugees – resting, stranded, or moving slowly, sometimes in different directions – crowded the road. Icy patches and ruts made footing treacherous. The SS, an interpreter asserted, would shoot those who dropped out. I doubted that, but SS troops were not noted for their patience or compassion. Ruski P.O.W.'s, left to die or killed because they fell behind, adorned the ditches. I had no idea where we were. Did anybody? Or were we simply a bunch of forgotten kriegies, aimlessly trudging west because someone ordered our camp commander not to let the Russians free us? Singing had helped me keep going on maneuvers, so I tried that. It didn't work. A goal lay ahead then. Did it now, or was our group, as several suspected, traveling in a circle?

That evening, at a farm near Jastrow, we received soup, margarine and hot water. More soup arrived at daybreak. I needed it; with no Red Cross food except the D-bars, no bread, and no body fat to rely on, every mouthful of nourishment counted. Something delayed our departure; we waited in the cold, stomping our feet on the ground to promote circulation. I had wrapped my pajama bottoms around one boot and the tops around the other to prevent frostbite; it didn't do any good so I converted them to a covering for my face and neck. When my fingers, curled up in the gloves issued to me at Oflag 64, were about to freeze, I blew on them; or, sticking a hand through layers of clothing, held it against my skin.

We went 17 kilometers, to Zippnow. Straw in the barn kept us warm but no food was provided until dawn. Following a march of an hour or two we reached an abandoned stalag where, a guard stated, we would spend the night; our German commandant's car had been seized by higher-ranking officers and he was too tired to go farther. Stoves in the barracks, amply supplied with briquets for fuel, dried out our shoes and sox. Supper consisted of creamed carrots and sauerkraut and I "slept in a bunk on a mattress." Soup for breakfast was followed by a rumor that this might be another day of rest.

We'd been told more than once that kriegies who were sick or unable to continue for other reasons could stay behind. On at least one of those occasions arrangements had supposedly been made to transport them in boxcars. Though weakened by lack of food, I seemed to be okay: no frozen toes or fingers, no breathing problems from sleeping in straw-filled barns, no headaches or diarrhea. Of the 1300 or so who had left Oflag 64 together, a third were now gone, some by hiding or sneaking away, some as a result of disability. Keller, suffering from stomach pains, had dropped out. Sampson and Hawthorne were still with the group but I rarely saw either of them.

The anticipated day of rest failed to materialize. We were rounded up at noon, and due to taking a wrong turn arrived at Machlin, 12 kilometers from the stalag, "way after dark." Fifty of us went to a small barn. The owner furnished hot water. Mahoney cooked a rabbit he had traded for and let me have a bite. I ate one of my D-bars and before leaving the next morning wrote: "Morale (mine) poor, horrible march, bitter cold, great drifts, windswept plains, ruts in road, refugees."

It was important, I realized, not to despair. I sang *Blue Skies*, thinking this would lift my spirits. It didn't; my reaction was, "Get real!" Whispering, "When you're down and out, lift up your head and shout," helped a little. Again and again, forcing myself to put one foot in front of the other, I said to myself, "Another step, another step, keep going, keep going, we're nearly there." I recalled stories I'd read about people lost in snow storms. Some lay down and died; others made themselves go on and survived. I intended to be a survivor; to keep going, through will power, until my body wore out.

That afternoon I believed it finally had worn out. Frigid winds beat against me. My legs were like pieces of lead, my feet and fingers numb. The column halted; kriegies began sitting down. In the center of an intersection where two country roads crossed at right angles, shivering uncontrollably, I unbuttoned my coat, pulled it over my head, and lying in a fetal position hoped my exhaled breath would create warmth. My reserves were depleted, I concluded; my vital processes could no longer function. A truck driving on either road would probably hit me; I realized that but decided not to move. If I was about to die, it didn't matter how.

Shaking violently, I became aware of something pressing against a rib. It was my last D-bar, in a pocket of my field jacket. I grabbed it, ripped off the wrapper, and without hesitation ate the whole thing. When a guard yelled for us to start forward, I stood up, rearranged my coat, draped the blanket across my shoulder, and not shivering any more, plodded on. The crisis had passed.

In Templeburg we waited two hours while barns were located, then got hot water and soup. Whether the farmers and their families prepared the food we received during these stops, or somebody else had to, I didn't know. Usually it was good, but not always.

Our journey the following day lasted a couple of hours. We were sent to farms near Heinrichsdorf. Dinner consisted of milk fresh from the cows, bread, margarine, and "*beaucoups* macaroni." Sampson found me and asked for cigarettes; he needed them for trading. I could hardly bring myself to share my remaining pack and a half, but remembered his generosity at Oflag 64 and let him have the partially empty one.

In the morning additional bread was issued, and, before noon, additional soup. We went eight kilometers to Falkenburg. The next day, after a march of 17 kilometers, we reached Sulshagen, were given boiled potatoes and ersatz coffee for supper and taken to an abandoned school for the night. It was full of refugees, but our SS cadre cleared two rooms on the second floor for us to crowd into. We slept on our sides, each man's front against the adjacent one's back, uncomfortable but warm. The yard was the toilet; refugees – men, women and children – and P.O.W.'s responded there to nature's assorted calls. I tried not to look at the women beside me, and hoped civilized existence would soon return.

That evening, following a full day of marching, the goons obtained soup and boiled spuds for us. The next afternoon we arrived at Zeitlitz, having covered 22 kilometers, and again got soup and potatoes. Sampson heard that boxcars were in Ruhnow, seven kilometers away, to transport the sick. There being plenty of room, anybody could go. He planned to; what about me? Those who didn't would continue on foot.

It was a difficult decision. The march had been grim but things were better from the food standpoint, my health appeared to be okay, and I dreaded another trip like the horrible one from Limburg to Schubin. On the other hand, we might walk for a long,

long time in frigid weather, and who could say what food would be available tomorrow? A train had a destination; our column, apparently, didn't.

Or did it? Hawthorne, as a member of the S.A.O.'s staff, might have inside information. I located him and we talked for two or three minutes. Colonel Goode was staying with the group, so he would also. None of them knew anything. "It's a gamble either way," he said.

Anxious to make the right choice, I weighed the risks each involved, then, when the Ruhnow contingent lined up to leave, joined them. Marching from town to town along the backroads of eastern Germany appealed to me less than riding on a train that presumably would wind up somewhere.

Four boxcars were provided for a hundred and eighty of us, so we were able to shift around and take turns lying down. Meat was issued, one can per ten kriegies. I traded half of the bread I'd saved for some Klim.

We left at dawn, sandwiched into a westbound freight train. It stopped frequently and the guards often let us out. They did not, however, give us any food. I ate the last of my bread the second evening and had nothing the next day, which was spent on a siding at Stargard. In Pasewalk, the following afternoon, a Red Cross kitchen for refugees served us soup. My heart sank when they ran short, but more came and I received a generous portion. The misery that characterized our trip from Limburg wasn't present, but we were uncomfortable, bored, worried about being bombed or strafed by Allied planes, thirsty, and of course hungry.

On the fifth day we pulled into a huge railroad yard at the edge of Berlin. A guard, sliding our door open, instructed us not to get out; everybody immediately did. Curious about the freight cars behind us, I walked along them to the end of the train. A well-dressed, middle-aged civilian, crossing the tracks, saw me and said something in German. Raising my shoulders to indicate lack of understanding, I pointed to the others and responded, "Kriegsgefangener Americaner."

"Ah, that is unfortunate; it is a bad war," he replied in English, and went on.

Kraut soldiers were standing in the doors of boxcars on an adjacent track. Although it was strictly *verboten*, I sidled over to them and, holding up my last pack of Old Golds, asked, "Haben Sie Brod?" They conferred, and after considerable fumbling handed me a loaf of bread and three hard rolls. I tossed them the cigarettes and hastened away, aware that an officer or guard might at any moment shoot me.

We departed a couple of hours later and reached Luckenwalde, 30 miles to the south, that evening. Our guards, attempting to lead us to Stalag III-A, lost their way and backtracked twice before arriving at the gate about 9 p.m. We were taken to a building where 21 of us, including Hank Schainhorst and "Mac" McKittrick, two guys I'd met on the train ride, ended up in a cubicle of seven triple-deck bunks without slats or mattresses. Kriegies from a nearby barracks, hurrying over, informed us that at least 17,000 P.O.W.'s – British, Canadian, French, Russian, Polish, Danish, Norwegian and American – were in this camp. Each nationality had its own "compound," with enlisted men separated from officers. Ours included a latrine building and sports field – the latter now covered by snow – but no library or books nor any classes, theater, choir, band or other amenities.

A group from the English compound brought us hot water. I exchanged the last of my powdered milk for a teaspoonful of sugar and enough coffee to make one cup, which Hank, Mac and I shared. Hank had some meat; we ate that and Mac's remaining prunes, then "borrowed" enough coffee for another cup. "Our food is kaput," my notes state. The barracks wasn't heated, so the three of us slept together, my blanket on the floor, theirs on top.

We had appels at 9 and 4. Lieutenant Colonels Hagen and Monroe were our S.A.O.'s but we rarely saw Monroe; apparently he was sick much of the time. The goons provided soup, boiled potatoes and a little salt at noon; bread, coffee and a dab of margarine or sprinkling of sugar in the afternoon. We ate in our cubicles, and for the first week or so were too hungry to save anything for an evening snack or breakfast in the morning. The bread was soggy and tasted sour; putting a thin layer of margarine and sugar on it – or, if they were gone, a pinch of salt – made it more palatable. The coffee – ersatz, and completely flavorless –

helped fill our stomachs. Occasionally barley or oatmeal took the place of soup.

Diarrhea, which I'd avoided on the march and in the boxcar, caught up with me. Night after night, doing my best not to disturb Hank and Mac, I rushed from our makeshift bed to the latrine. A head cold kept my nose either clogged or dripping. I felt awful and spent many hours wrapped in a blanket, trying to regain strength and stay warm.

On February 19th, nine days after our arrival, the Danes gave us Red Cross parcels from their supply, each of them to be divided among five men. My allotment consisted of thin slices of salami, cheese and *knachebrod*; some butter, sugar and candy; and a sizable portion of cocoa powder. The cartons were fuel for our Smokey Joes, acquired from the British, so we could toast the bread and heat held-back spuds. The goons issued everybody a spoonful of ersatz honey and, three days later, a sliver of horsemeat. Despite these welcome additions, my stomach continually felt empty. Once, noticing a cubicle mate about to discard coffee grounds he had used many times, I asked for them and brewed a cup for Hank, Mac and me.

The kriegie who built an unauthorized radio at Oflag 64 brought it to Luckenwalde and listened regularly to BBC broadcasts. Our troops appeared to be advancing despite dogged but sporadic resistance.

Slats were eventually furnished, and straw-stuffed burlap mattresses, so we could sleep in the bunks. I chose a top one because the building would be warmer near the ceiling. Each of us got a second blanket. With a borrowed razor I hacked off my beard. The diarrhea, having exhausted me, exhausted itself — temporarily, anyway — so that dashing to the latrine was no longer necessary.

On March 9th, as I lay in bed at daybreak, a gentle breeze, coming through an open window, blew across my face. It seemed to signify that winter had ended and spring, nature's season of regeneration and renewal, was beginning. I hoped so; my weakened body needed regenerating. Diarrhea had sapped what little strength remained in it.

That afternoon everyone received a No. 10. Five days later we received another and were told that they could be expected weekly, at least for awhile. I traded cigarettes for a notebook and started writing:

> *Weds., Mar. 14: Paper again; I can resume keeping a record of events. The news has grown more encouraging almost daily. On Febr. 27th, when the members of my cubicle were forming a pool, I picked March 31st as the date of our liberation. It was the most optimistic choice and the others kidded me. But they were changing their minds before long as we learned of Allied advances, Kraut disorganization, and beaucoups prisoners. Today things are every bit as bright, but with March 31st drawing closer and our troops pausing for pre-planned crossings of the Rhine, I realize that there is a lot to be done before Germany is finally overrun, which apparently will be required. I haven't lost faith, though, and expect the war to end by the middle of April and myself to be enjoying 30 days leave in Lincoln by June or July. Maybe this is wishful thinking; some are saying two, three or even six months. Well, we shall see.*
>
> *Thurs., Mar. 15: Soup came at 1, and it was grass soup -- the first time we've had that at Luckenwalde – and what horrible stuff! But it's food, and I ate mine and part of Mac's, supplementing with cheese sandwiches. For a few minutes I was filled; indeed, for a few minutes I had a stomach ache. Both feelings were soon gone and I returned from my half hour of exercise outdoors to bash some more. . . .*
>
> *Fri., Mar. 16: Walked awhile in the afternoon, it being a beautiful clear spring day. The waves of bombers we saw yesterday were 1,350 strong, aiming at targets east of Berlin. Had a demi-tasse and then got ready for my evening meal. We were given a spud issue today (our first since Tuesday) plus one-sixth loaf of bread, two spoonfuls of cottage cheese, and a spoonful of bully beef. Fried the bully and a little Prem I had left. The spuds were small; I browned them whole, making gravy out of grease, oleo, Klim and bread crumbs. It was swell. For dessert, a prune soggy – almost as good as those raisin kriegies I used to make at Schubin. . . .*

"Demi-tasse" meant half a cup of coffee. Hank, Mac and I took turns heating the water. Our supply of cardboard for fuel being limited, we didn't heat much at a time, and joked that having a demi-tasse placed us among the socially elite. A soggy was bread chunks soaked in powdered milk, with prunes or chocolate added. The word "kriegie" had two meanings; it referred to a P.O.W. and also to a milk and sugar batter with jam or raisins stirred in.

> *March 18: Mac roused me at 8 with my coffee cup half full of hot water, so I began the day sitting in bed drinking a demi-tasse. Breakfast consisted of bread crusts, cheese, and when the goons brought the heise, a full cup of coffee. After appel, walked around, then – hooray! – our parcels. Mine wasn't exactly my favorite, so I decided to trade for some items I prefer. I swapped my sardines for tuna; my oleo for a D-bar; that D-bar for pineapple jam to make tastier kriegies; my coffee for peanut butter; my last week's luncheon meat for coffee and six biscuits; that coffee for more peanut butter; my prunes for biscuits; a D-bar for one-fourth can of milk powder; a D-bar for one-half can of cocoa. When this wild spree was over I had a very satisfied feeling, though I may have been a bit too generous. At noon we got pea soup. In the afternoon I strolled around for my half hour of exercise. . . . Although we have no classes and there is nothing to read, the days seem to pass fairly quickly and the spring-like weather helps immeasurably. We're sweating out a move, for the Russians are apparently only 40 or 50 miles away; but a move in this weather wouldn't be as bad as before and we would probably go to an established camp where the rest of our old Schubin bunch is located. Viewing the military situation objectively and free of wishful thinking, I pick May 15 - 31 for the end of the war, thus allowing 4 to 6 weeks for buildup along the Rhine and 2 to 3 for the final drives into Germany. Secretly, though, I hope for April.*

The "rest of our old Schubin bunch" marched for another month after we split off from them, and wound up in a camp near Hammelburg.

It was rumored that Hitler had authorized commanders of all stalags to shoot prisoners of war, or starve them to death, in retaliation for Allied bombers killing German civilians. Mac's response was, "What's new about that; they're already starving us." Bryant thought the goons ought to conserve their bullets for use against the Russians. We didn't let the rumor worry us, but it was a poignant reminder that we were not yet free.

Books brought to Luckenwalde by individual kriegies began circulating; in the weeks that followed I read *Of Mice and Men*, *Death Comes for the Archbishop*, *Evidence of Things Seen*, a world history and several mystery stories. We also started a bridge tournament with our well-worn deck of cards.

Monday, March 19, 9:15 a.m. I am sitting on the edge of my bunk, waiting for appel. Hank is below me – my feet are probably hanging in his face. Mac is bashing a not too tasty looking bread and prune soggy. Cortez is shining his shoes with our shoe brush, acquired from a guard for ten cigs. O'Donnell is examining himself in a mirror we found. Botts sits cross-legged, reading a pocket book. Bradley is on his bunk spooning out Klim for a bash of some kind. Mulder, Hillman and Roberts are talking; so are Underwood, Alesio and Klopp. Plummer and Tietje are discussing the food value of oleo. We're a congenial group, for which I am thankful since in these crowded conditions any friction would make life most unpleasant. I owe much to Hank's good nature because now and then one of my slats drops on his bed, chaff from my burlap tick floats down on him and his belongings, my combat boots leave a blob of dirt on his blanket whenever I step on it to get up to my bed, and every so often a scrap of bread or potato or the like slips from my fingers and falls in his lap. My health is good, for which I am certainly grateful. Once in awhile my stomach hurts, but since that lengthy siege of diarrhea after we first arrived here I've felt okay.

5 p.m. Appel is over and it will soon be my turn on the stove. This morning I walked a little, then made a serviceable but far from fancy plate for myself out of two empty oleo tins. Soup was straight barley, very popular because of its similarity to oatmeal; and when I added sugar, milk and raisins it tasted great. The bread ration dropped to 1/7th loaf and we got no spuds but I had some saved from yesterday. . . .

Tuesday, March 20: . . . I am listening to the bevy of new rumors. The best is that the war has ended. It's the first time we've heard this. Rumor No. 2: the Nazi party is no longer in control. No. 3: parcels Saturday instead of Monday. No. 4: parcels Thurs. or Fri. O'Donnell is so sure of it he will bet two D-bars. However, they're all rumors and we have nothing official at all. Despite the probabilities of no parcel until Monday (and perhaps only one more after that – Rumor No. 5), I've bashed well, and I decided this afternoon that it's better to bash heavily and feel half-way satisfied than to spread it out and never lose the food craving. . . . Bombers dot the sky, some leaving vapor trails behind them, others not but glistening in the sun. Ten days until my date for our liberation.

Thursday, March 22: Another beautiful day. Spent three hours waiting to use the stove and trying to appease my growing hunger by bits of bread dabbed with paté and cheese or peanut butter. Mac, Hank, Bradley and I talked about the war – with Patton at the Rhine, the First Army across, and a 40-mile smokescreen along the northern front, it should be over soon. We discussed our chances to live if Kraut guerillas seize this area, and the possibility of internal collapse in Germany that might lead to angry mobs attacking us.

Saturday, March 24: This morning I found two lice in my hair, so those little bastards are back to torture me, I guess. The bedbugs are biting, and I have lumps on my face, neck and arms. Up three times last night to visit the latrine.

Sunday, March 25: . . . The bird reported four new crossings of the Rhine – two British, one Canadian, one our Ninth Army – so we all pulled out the parcels for a celebration bash. Had cocoa (rich and thick) and a biscuit with jam, two squares of a D-bar, and a demi-tasse. We've been getting our goon issue of sugar (one spoonful) almost every day, but the margarine comes pretty irregularly. Got spuds for the third afternoon in a row. Appel time now. Special flash from the bird: Patton has crossed the Rhine. Hurry, boys, hurry.

Thus the days passed. Our ordeal, though not yet over, appeared to be nearing an end. "Plagued by itching," I noted on March 26th. The night of the 29th was "bad because of the bugs." We were given a salve that supposedly would (and perhaps did) help. The lice eventually departed; my cold and the stuffed up or runny nose finally did too. Spring weather warmed our bodies, which for months had been chilled.

Reports from the bird continued to be encouraging. "Patton is headed this way," I wrote. In a bull session regarding what might happen after our return to the States, most of the group felt that long-time kriegies would probably be discharged and that no ex-kriegies would be sent to the Pacific.

Some of the guys think people at home won't believe us when we talk about life as a P.O.W. My initial reaction was that there isn't anything about this life they wouldn't believe; but then, recalling our boxcar rides, the march through Poland, and the first weeks here, I decided that the misery they brought may be beyond belief. Also, there is something about kriegie life in general that people at home may not be able to comprehend, something that makes it restless and unsure. Being a prisoner of war isn't all basking in the sun, playing bridge, eating Red Cross food and shooting the bull. Night always comes, and with it the realization that in spite of these good things you are controlled by a desperate, unpredictable enemy and existing on a starvation diet. That's the best I can express it.

Optimism is still prevalent. My cubicle mates turn to me when the bird finishes and say, "Looks like we're going to pay you, Steve." That March 31st date will be a lot closer than many of them anticipated.

"I think the war will end in a few days, if not in a few hours, if it is not already over," my March 29th entry declares:

The advances in the west, the prisoners captured, the confusion and utter disorganization of the Krauts, plus the 1,001 rumors circulating through our barracks, have gone to my head. Everyone is talking constantly about the end. The bird at 5:45, right after appel, spoke of Allied forces moving toward Nuremberg, Munster and Kassell; of fighter pilots seeing no enemy, no roadblocks, no anything ahead of our troops. Rumor has it that Kesselring is negotiating with Eisenhower, that the Wehrmacht has taken over from Hitler, that Allied advances not yet reported by our commanders are breath-taking. Mulder says paratroopers will land here to protect us. One thing is certain: much is happening . . .

By April 1st, Easter Sunday, I was "back down to earth." Each of us got a No.10, from which we planned to enjoy, on the day of our liberation, "the most tremendous bash known to man."

April 2: . . . My food situation is good in all except sugar. I have no crackers but can stretch the daily one-eighth loaf of goon bread, and we still receive a spoonful of sugar every so often. The week should be okay as far as my eating is concerned; and even if we have to go ten days on the present parcel, I can get along.

April 4: . . . Our bread ration dropped to 1/10th loaf today, but we had hunks of horsemeat in the soup. . . . Further cuts in rations are hinted at, so we're living almost entirely on the parcels, which means darn little food. However, it's tasty food and it provides variety. Ordinarily I would save some each week in order to build up a reserve; but with the end of kriegie life apparently so near, it seems foolish to deny myself the food I need and crave. And yet when I do bash, as yesterday, I'm no more satisfied than when I don't. If I could eat at definite times and limit myself to a pre-planned amount, it would be great. I've done this occasionally. . . .

April 5th, my last chance to win the pool, slipped by uneventfully. After having a kriegie cut my hair, I shaved, then used the cupful of lukewarm water to bathe. "Lord but I'm dirty, and in spite of my soaping and scrubbing, I didn't get very clean." Water dripped from the faucet extremely slowly and was ice cold; heating it on a Smokey Joe consumed valuable fuel.

"All is well," April 9th's entry comments,

and though we are far from pessimistic, the abundant optimism of Easter weekend is gone. The BBC reports relate primarily to the huge numbers of Kraut prisoners; news regarding advances is scarce, either because of censorship or because our troops are consolidating. Surely the end will come soon. . . . Alesio gave me a pack of Sir Walter pipe tobacco for a box of prunes, so I smoked that instead of cigarette butts. What a difference. Played Poker for 3 hours and won again. Tietje now owes me 15 cigs.

Packages from home addressed to Oflag 64 were delivered to Stalag III-A. We gathered near the end of one barracks while a member of the S.A.O.'s staff called out names. Assuming mine would be one of them, I pressed forward. Unfortunately, it wasn't. Each of us had been allowed to turn in the name of a kriegie not at Luckenwalde and claim his. I designated Austin, but there were none for him either. All of us shared those that remained, which is how Alesio acquired the Sir Walter Raleigh.

We were told that the Americans in this camp might be transferred to Moosburg:

This was a most unpleasant bit of news, to say the least. Here's hoping Patton, or somebody, reaches Luckenwalde before we depart, because a boxcar ride or march or truck ride, especially in these days of short rations and beaucoups strafing and bombing, is not my choice of activities.

"The British officers," I noted on April 11th, "are supposed to leave today in boxcars, with their NCO's tomorrow, and us on Friday."

April 12: The British kept themselves from being moved out on schedule, and by their antics are now causing additional delay. I admire how adept they are at screwing things up for our German guards. Every minute of delay helps.

The bird was swell – Allies nearing Leipzig, 50 miles from Czechoslovakia, 70 miles from Berlin; the Ruski's starting their movement west. It's 90% certain we won't leave, and it looks like both liberation and the end of the war are rapidly approaching. While getting ready for bed I heard planes overhead, so slipped on my boots and coat and went outside. Flares were descending on Berlin. Searchlights scanned the sky; once in awhile their beams crossed the bottom of a bomber or the vapor trail behind it. Bombs exploded every few seconds. It was a short raid, and before long the all clear was sounding.

At noon on the 13th we were told that President Roosevelt had died. Despite my Republican heritage, I was saddened and wondered how his death would affect our country and the war. Twelve P-47's and four P-38's strafed and dive-bombed south of us. I watched until they disappeared from sight. "No news but the story is that fighting is taking place less than 50 miles from here."

Sat., Apr. 14, 10 a.m.: This is my "semi-anniversary" – half a year as a kriegie. So far I've done no celebrating. We should get our #10's today. And hell, we might even be liberated today. Last night's bird said allies are seven miles south of Leipzig, 27 miles from Czech border; and in a special announcement this morning Col. Hagen described the conflicting reports he's received regarding this camp and the surrounding area: (1) that Germany has declared it a neutral zone; (2) that the guards have been ordered to defend it, which they intend to do by firing a volley of shots into the air and then leaving. It's a clear day, slightly chilly but the sun should warm us.

Cortez was making sketches that depicted important events in his life as a P.O.W. I decided to try my hand at it, and using the back of an empty carton spent several hours on a drawing called "Six Months of Kriegie Daze."

"The end is now so near," I wrote, "that expectation keeps us keyed up." Allied planes had bombed the marshalling yards in Potsdam, ten miles north of Luckenwalde, the previous evening. "What a magnificent spectacle: flak, searchlights, explosions, flares, tracers, flames, concussion; and all so close it seemed to be in our own backyard."

"News not so good," a short April 16th entry asserts. The 17th's says, "Still very definitely a kriegie," and observes that "beaucoups German Folke-Wulffs were in the air," and "we can hear what sounds like artillery fire."

Our bird reported Ruski movement toward Berlin, and told of American troops at Leipzig, Magdeburg, across the Elbe, and seven miles from Nuremberg. Liberation soon, yes, but perhaps not for another week or so – I'm definitely down to earth again! I got cigs, razor blades, two packages of noodle soup mix, and a pack of pipe tobacco from unclaimed parcels. Sold my cheese for 60 cigs and combined all cigs to buy a can of Klim from a Polish officer for 200. Played Bridge, then walked around outside and watched planes diving in the distance to strafe or bomb. After supper I visited with guys from Cubicle 2.

We were informed that the supply of No. 10's was depleted, "except for possibly one-fifth on Saturday."

Wed., Apr. 18: Slept well. Breakfast of coffee only – have to cut down because no more parcels, and experience shows it may be awhile before we are liberated. A swell day, so I'll try to soak up some sun. I am filthy – my skin has a very visible layer of greasy, grimy dirt on it which cold water won't remove and hot does only partially. I have bites all over me, including several on my ears that are painful. Many of them are infected. The lice have disappeared.

8:15 p.m.: Ah, what a pleasant surprise this afternoon – Austin received a parcel from home and Austin was the one whose name I submitted in claiming the packages of absentees. Contents:

2 pr. heavy sox	*Wool sweater*
3 handkerchiefs	*Cotton shirt and shorts*
Peanuts (salted)	*1 box soda crackers*
Caramels	*Coffee*

Pecans	*60 chicken bouillon cubes*
15 tea bags	*30 beef bouillon cubes*
Figs	*1 box veg. noodle soup*
6 vitamin candy bars	*1 lb. sugar*

I gave everybody in the cubicle two bouillon cubes, an additional four apiece to Hank and Mac, and ten to Sampson plus a couple of tea bags. Traded part of my noodle soup for oatmeal. . . . About thirty B-26's flew by, very low, with escort of P-47's. The signs of war, and the sounds, are close. A sergeant captured 11 miles from here assured us that allied troops are coming. So, a fig, a handful of peanuts and two caramels as another evening fades away. Thanks, Austie!

Having completed "Six Months of Kriegie Daze," I started a drawing entitled "From Lincoln to Luckenwalde" that reflected my two years of active duty, since April, 1943, and for a few minutes thought about those carefree days in the library building. A lot of ground had been covered since then, both literally and figuratively. Things had not turned out as expected, but surely the worst was now behind me.

No Allies yet, but hundreds of B-17's. Smoke to the southeast and explosions in the distance. My food (I'm stretching) will last through this week easily, but next week I'll sweat if Americans or Ruskis don't arrive.

Never before had I seen so many B-17's. They flew in V's, silhouetted against the cloudless blue sky, the droning of their engines clearly audible. Fighter planes accompanied them, but no enemy aircraft appeared nor any opposition from the ground.

Word came the following morning that the entire camp

would be marched out today, probably to Berlin where a final stand is being made. We got busy at once on ways to delay them, and I developed plans for escape. I'm not going to Berlin with the Allies this near. However, it's 5:30 and there's no sign of activity, so I guess it won't happen today. And surely every day must count. . . . 800 heavy bombers with large fighter escort bombed on three sides of us.

Sat., Apr. 21, 1:15 p.m.: I am not liberated but things close to liberation are occurring. Goons with full field packs and suitcases are departing, though guards still pace along the wire fence. The Ruski's are roaming around and a white flag hangs from their barracks. I don't know who put it up or what it means. We hear artillery and smoke is visible to the north and east. It's rumored that a Russian infantry unit has reached Luckenwalde. . . . I could not help but think, while heating my pudding, that not far from us soldiers are suffering and dying while, almost in their midst, we cook puddings. That's life, perhaps, but I and many others owe much to those who continue to fight.

6:15: The situation has clarified somewhat. The goon commandant turned the camp over to a Norwegian general, the senior Allied officer, and moved all Krauts outside the fences. They are digging in by the main gate. I was sent to the goon barracks to prevent looting, but took advantage of the short time I had there to loot it myself, as did the rest. I acquired a bottle of grenadine, a bayonet, bread, onions, a notebook, goon belt buckle, flashlight, and some medals. More time would have yielded more loot, but we were called back. The Russians are acting like little kids let out of school early. Four of them have a car and are driving it up and down the street; another has a bicycle and is showing off. They have broken into the potato warehouse and carried away bags of spuds. For awhile (and maybe still) they were begging for cigarettes, which American officers tossed across the fence to them. Not all of their actions have been innocent; they got into our storage area and made off with three bags of private parcels, then disarmed a goon and dragged him away. The British and Americans are manning the gates and doing guard duty, the French are strolling around, everybody is wondering what will happen. With artillery sounding nearby, goons digging foxholes, and no sign of Allied soldiers, I certainly don't feel liberated or particularly at ease. . . .

In the goon barracks I came across the Nazi flag that flew above our compound each day. This would be a great memento of Stalag III-A, I decided, and stuck it inside my shirt to bring home.

Sunday, April 22, 10:15 a.m.: Awakened at 7 by the cry, "Hey, there's a Russian armored vehicle outside." Mulder says it arrived about 4 a.m. The commander told him they needed to leave while he could still get back to his lines, that his army is only 4 miles from here, that they are killing all Krauts they encounter, that many Ruskis are coming and we will then see the Red Army in action.

When the armored car left it was fired on by German troops. Liberation is close but we are still kriegsgefangeners.

Last night a plane flew over us with guns blazing. It was strafing the goons, but the empty cartridge cases falling on our roof made us fear we were the target. Four Russian fighters went by this morning, but now German FW's seem to be controlling the skies. There is fighting near the main gate – lots of small arms fire.

11:30: And so, finally, liberation. Shouts filled the air and I beheld a beautiful sight: 6 or 8 Ruski tanks lumbering down our street, large tanks with infantrymen riding on them. Behind the tanks came truckloads of soldiers, waving and smiling, but grim fighters nevertheless. Some were mere boys of 14 or 15, wearing tattered uniforms but part of the mighty Russian army. Most of their equipment was American, and the planes overhead were our P-39's even though they bore the Red Star insignia. We passed around cigarettes; they took them eagerly and tried to talk to us. The column of trucks stayed awhile, then drove on. The Ruski prisoners, after emotionally shaking hands with their comrades, marched off, followed by the tanks. A Russian unit is outposting the camp, so we can feel a little safer. As a symbol of our liberation they drove a tank across the high barbed wire fence (accidentally pulling down our power lines in the process).

For us to be free is wonderful, yet even more wonderful is the news that the Ruskis are well into Berlin. Surprisingly, my joy at being liberated is less than my joy that this terrible war appears to be ending. I am free, but what I yearn for, as do people throughout the world, is peace. Still no water. I've hit the latrine five times; feel okay though. Finished Lincoln to Luckenwalde.

7 p.m.: The Russians are in Luckenwalde, we've heard, where they're drunkenly driving cars, firing their guns and raping women. We, meanwhile, remain in or near our barracks. Artillery shells are landing close by, and Ruski anti-aircraft is blasting away at FW's that are strafing them. A Ruski officer will be in charge of us until administrative contact is made with U.S. forces. Tactical contact has already been made. We are to be evacuated by the Americans.

Tues., Apr. 24, 2:15: I spent yesterday in bed – diarrhea and stomach cramps. Several visits to the latrine, then to the dispensary. They gave me paregoric, which I threw up. I managed to keep down some pills. At 7, a cup of tea, my first food or drink since Sunday. Apparently the Germans have left this area. All is quiet save for the sound of distant firing and Russian P-39's and Stormoviks cruising above us. We are sore at the French for being uncooperative, and at our own officers because of reveille at 7, lack of chow and unnecessary restrictions. Our Red Cross food is about gone, our bread ration is one-tenth instead of one-eighth. The French are cooking all kinds of stuff in the kitchen and right now are sauntering by with No. 10's. No word from the Yanks.

Memories of liberation shortly after our departure from Schubin, when, told to sit tight, we ended up being de-liberated, didn't instill confidence in the senior officers who presumably were looking out for us. Neither did seeing the French carrying our No. 10's under their arms. I considered leaving, but most of the others weren't, and it seemed like the best course of action was to stick together and be repatriated in an orderly manner. Hopefully our S.A.O.'s knew what they were doing.

The Canadians contributed food parcels to us, one for each four men. We split some of the items and drew straws for the rest. I put my share of the butter and marmalade on a biscuit and wrote, "Boy, is it good to taste real butter."

Weds., Apr. 25th, 9 a.m.: Walked around awhile, then climbed up into a guard tower and gazed at the surrounding terrain. It was an amazing sight, for in every direction columns of smoke rose from fires that are wiping away German towns and cities. To the north, where the Ruskis are fighting in Potsdam and Berlin, smoke spread across the horizon. A BBC correspondent said Germany is a nation committing suicide. How true that is. . . .

A goon plane flew over last night, strafing, but I didn't wake up. Things are quiet now except for an occasional FW, which draws Russian anti-aircraft. Our water was on for 15 minutes this morning and may be on again at noon. . . .

The days go by more slowly than ever. French P.O.W.'s wearing G I uniforms are in Luckenwalde, living off the fat of the land. Some Americans are too (enlisted men), and many Ruskis. Our instructions from Hagen are to stay here.

Another private parcel just arrived for our cubicle to share and it has lots of chocolate. A few of the boys got letters – gosh, what I wouldn't give for one. Oh well, I have enough food and will be home soon. What a great day that will be!

It would be great, all right, but less so if dad was dead. I'd heard nothing from Sampson regarding my family and had received no letters, cards or packages from them or anyone else.

Hank got a "Dear John" letter. The girl he was engaged to wrote that she'd been dating a navy officer and planned to marry him. Though crushed, he took it philosophically — "What else can I do?" — and let me read her explanation. She would always have deep affection for him, it said, but the months of being alone (Hank had been a prisoner since 1943) took their toll on her.

"They don't think about the toll these months have taken on us, do they?" I commented, trying to be helpful.

"She doesn't realize that, Steve. It's okay, I forgive her. I'll start over when the war ends — find someone new."

I, too, would be starting over, seeking someone new, probably a younger girl since those my age were no doubt already married. What if the younger ones aren't interested in a fellow 24 years old? They might not be. Who knows what things will be like when we get home? Will we be strangers in our own land?

The warmth most of us felt for the Russians after their troops liberated Stalag III-A had chilled. The soldiers they left to guard us took watches from kriegies who'd traded for them; and in at least one case, when the kriegie resisted, threatened him with an automatic rifle. When I was in the guard tower surveying the surrounding area, a Ruski with a gun came over and stood at the base of it. I saw him and waved. He didn't wave back or smile, and sauntered away after I departed.

Somebody in the barracks acquired a radio. Listening to recordings by the Glenn Miller, Les Brown and Jimmy Dorsey bands led me to write:

People in America are dancing and laughing and having fun. That's fine; I don't begrudge them their happy moments one bit, but it makes me realize – for the first time, I guess – the extent of my sacrifices compared to those who didn't leave.

From 10 tonight until 6 a.m. tomorrow I'm to be on duty as a guard. That will change my routine. We are moving to the Adolph Hitler Lager, a rest camp for German officers six miles away. The Russian commandant thinks conditions at Stalag III-A are awful. I agree, but wish we were going home instead. Well, it can't be long – I hope.

It was, though – longer, anyway, than I'd anticipated.

Thurs., May 3, 11 a.m.: The days creep by. We have stood reveille while artillery shells whizzed above our heads, explosions rocked our buildings, and tracers flew in plain sight. During the night the fighting near our camp was heaviest, I walked "C" patrol alone and unarmed. The Adolph Hitler Lager is now out of the question – overrun by Ruskis and refugees. I am a mass of bites and covered with grime. We have seen no Yanks and heard from none. I'm tired as hell of soup, spuds and goon bread. My digestive system is shot; I have intestinal cramps, sour stomach, heartburn and runny bowels. The firing around us has stopped, so apparently this pocket of German resistance is kaput. Hitler is supposedly dead, the Krauts in Italy have surrendered, Berlin has fallen. Nerves are strained and the AWOL list is tremendous. A majority of the officers are staying because we've been ordered to and the S.A.O. has threatened to court martial for desertion anyone who takes off.

So here I am, living a life of utter ease, a free man but far from content; indeed, this seems to be the most difficult period since kriegie life began. Though conditions have certainly been far worse many times since October 14th, I expected it then and hardened myself to it. Now, with liberation a reality, the end of the war a matter of hours, and home so close, my protective armor is eroding. And yet it isn't; I just need to pour out my troubles and this diary is the place to do it. I'm trying to be optimistic and patient and see the good side of what's happening, but it's a crappy life.

Sat., May 5th, 11 a.m.: Officers from the 83rd Division arrived yesterday in two reconnaissance cars and said they would have transports take us to Wittenberg. Hagen told them we couldn't be ready until afternoon. The English want to be included and so do the Norwegians and all of this has to be cleared with the Ruskis. As a result we are still waiting. However, 23 ambulances came for the Americans who are hospitalized, and the 6 x 6's that delivered rations took out 120 of our G I's. The situation is hectic – people

> *leaving in droves, lack of food, antagonism toward our own and British commanders, and the screwed up way things are in general.*

Vehicles from the Ninth Army evacuated our remaining enlisted men and some officers, but none from my barracks. It developed that the Russians intended to "register" the rest of us and conduct our evacuation in front of newsreel cameras. "I am free but there's a doubly strong guard of Ruskis by the fences, armed with tommy guns and not hesitant about firing them. Many who slipped away have been brought back."

The next morning, fed up with obeying orders, I rolled under the barbed wire when nobody was looking, sneaked through a wooded area, and when I eventually emerged from it, saw three U. S. Army trucks parked beside a road. I raced over and climbed into one. The driver started forward but was quickly halted by armed Ruskis who made him return me to camp.

The war in Europe ended on May 8th. We listened to victory celebrations in America, to the Jack Benny, Bob Hope, and Bing Crosby programs, to dance bands playing popular songs; heard Churchill proclaim that all English P.O.W.'s would be out of Germany within a week; and watched Norwegians being evacuated. "None of this," my diary comments sarcastically, "added to our contentment." Fleas "devoured" me; "woke up 3 or 4 times tossing and turning from my beaucoups bites." Twice, in the icy water of our Sportsplatz pond, I swam for exercise and, using soap, attempted to get clean.

One afternoon my wanderings took me to where dead kriegies were buried. Most were Russians, in communal graves 10 feet across and 35 feet or so in length that originally must have been deep. An average of three per day died of starvation, we learned, because Ruski P.O.W.'s received no Red Cross food. Disease claimed others. A thin layer of soil covered the bodies but I could see their outlines, and in places an arm or a leg protruded. It was obvious that these prisoners had not been carefully laid to rest; they'd been thrown in – "dumped, as if they were garbage" – hundreds of them, maybe thousands. A wooden cross with a carved figure of Jesus had been erected nearby. Beyond it, on what appeared to be a grave, a smaller cross said, "Englische - Flieger - namen unbekant." I realized that of the millions to whom death had come as a result of the war, these were only a few — "a drop in the bucket" — but they seemed like a lot to me. To me one man, Thompson, had seemed like a lot.

The bugs kept up their torture. "Two nights ago," I noted on May 15th, "they were so bad I went outside to sleep but it was too cold. Slept out last night and slept okay."

On May 19th, writing for first time since the 15th, I described the intervening days as "much the same":

> *We get cheese at noon, seconds on soup, and occasionally peas, beans or sauerkraut. In the evening four of us play cards, then have cornstarch pudding with milk and sugar. It's an unpleasant life -- our bellies bloated, no butter or margarine for the bread, no toilet paper, nothing to do. Oh well, it's not unbearable and I'm not particularly hungry. The bugs are terrible and the stink of the overflowing latrine permeates everywhere. So it goes.*

That was my final entry. Below it I copied the last verse of a poem I'd read:

> *Stone walls do not a prison make,*
> *Nor iron bars a cage.*
> *Minds innocent and quiet take*
> *That for an hermitage.*
> *If I have freedom in my love*
> *And in my soul am free,*
> *Angels alone that soar above*
> *Enjoy such liberty.*
> *Richard Lovelace*
> *To Althea from Prison*

It's easier to suffer, to endure privation and discomfort, if you think there's a reason for it. While the fighting continued I accepted my lot stoically, conscious of how lucky I was compared to those in the front lines. Now, with the war over, aware of the fun our victorious troops were having and the celebrations at home, kriegie existence became harder to accept. Our senior officers assured us we would be evacuated soon by American forces and were better off sitting tight until they arrived. Trying to be good soldiers, most of us stayed, tolerating as patiently as one could expect under the circumstances — but with growing anger — detention by our Russian allies. Stone walls do not a prison make. Liberation from the Ruskis was bound to come.

It finally did, on Sunday, May 20th. Vehicles with the Red Star on them lined up to transport us to the Elbe, where U. S. personnel would be standing by. Carrying my diaries, notes, drawings, Nazi flag and miscellaneous items in a knapsack fashioned from the pajamas Sampson gave me, I boarded one of them, tremendously thankful to be leaving. Oflag 64 had been a decent place; Luckenwalde was a pit. The diarrhea and sour stomach that were so often present, the filthiness of my clothes, the vermin that continually infested both them and me, the grime I couldn't remove from my body, and the frustration that arose from not being released after V-E Day, made my imprisonment there both disagreeable and demeaning.

We rode past torn-up fields and battle-scarred towns to where the Elbe flowed peacefully through the greening countryside. A foot bridge had been built by our Corps of Engineers. We went across it single file. I didn't look back. Kriegie life was over. At last I was truly free.

9

The officers and enlisted men waiting on the other side cheered, saluted, and shook our hands as if we were heroes. The sincerity of their welcome pleased me immensely and I beamed my appreciation.

We rode in two-and-a-half-ton trucks, joking and laughing like Cub Scouts on a holiday outing, to Halle. There a lieutenant announced that our clothing and everything we had with us must be burned. A sympathetic NCO let me lay aside my writings and souvenirs for later retrieval. He was pouring gasoline on the rest as I walked, stark naked, to the delousing building, where we were given soap, shampoo, ointments to kill whatever creatures inhabited our skin or hair, and the privilege of prolonged hot showers. I emerged feeling clean for the first time in more than eight months, shaved, and donned brand new GI clothes furnished by the supply sergeant.

A medical officer explained that our stomachs were not capable of handling an onslaught of food, so for a few days we would be limited to small, specially-prepared meals supplemented by "health cocktails," a mixture of milk, eggs and vitamins. "General Eisenhower has directed that all P.O.W.'s be sent to the States as quickly as possible," he told us. "My job is to get you in shape for the trip." That sounded great.

A Red Cross mobile canteen showed up with doughnuts and

coffee. Officers, non-coms and privates gathered around it, then every one of them stepped away so we could go first. Standing in the warm sunshine, sipping coffee brewed from grounds that had never been used before, I realized how little it takes to make a person happy.

We ate dinner in a mess hall, seated on wooden benches at long tables. The food was excellent and my stomach had no trouble adjusting to it. Our health cocktails provided additional enjoyment. The barracks they assigned us to was neat and clean, with metal cots and real mattresses.

The following morning I wrote to my parents:

Dear folks,

If I don't reach Lincoln before this note does I'll be very disappointed. But just in case, be assured that I am well and rapidly regaining weight lost as a result of somewhat deficient German rations. We were evacuated from Luckenwalde yesterday and are now under American jurisdiction at Halle. Art Sampson is here and he is fine. We expect to be shipped home soon and are hoping for extended furloughs. Gosh but it's wonderful to eat army chow again.

I've written several times but don't suppose my letters got through. None of yours caught up with me. How I want to see you all and know that everything is okay. . . .

So relax in case you've been worried about your prisoner son, and start shining up the cocktail shaker.

Love,
Bill

There wasn't much to do, but that didn't matter. We participated in group calesthenics, played softball, walked to regain strength and build up our bodies, read *Stars and Stripes*, and went to a movie. "Being clean makes a world of difference," I noted in a pocket-size memo book I bought at the PX.

We also talked about the war with soldiers stationed at Halle. A few of them had been in Europe since D-Day, but most were replacements who arrived after that. "I came to France in December," a fellow named Murphy said, "and was sent to a unit fighting near Bastogne. The squad leader put me in a foxhole with a BAR man who'd been there awhile. Three days later he was killed. I figured I'd be next but I was too cold and scared and lonely to care."

"January was worse," another GI remarked, "because we had to advance through snow that was 18 inches deep. The trucks couldn't get to us with our blankets and food. I stomped my feet all one night to keep them from freezing. The next morning we were told to attack a Kraut outpost. Everybody was exhausted and a lot of guys were sick, but we did it. Our captain led us forward and fought beside me. He sure was a good officer."

A sergeant mentioned having a cocky, self-centered platoon leader who considered himself God's gift to the military. "He was yelling at us when a bullet hit him between the eyes and his body crumpled to the ground. Much as I hated the guy, that bothered me. I'd seen plenty of people flopping around and moaning and eventually dying, but this was the only time I ever saw someone alive and half a second later dead. I thought, "Hell, what's the use of trying? They'll get me too. They'll get us all."

A corporal nicknamed Tex was in college when the army assigned his ASTP group to an infantry division. "I came overseas with them but got hurt in a jeep accident and didn't rejoin the outfit until February. By then most of my buddies were gone – killed, wounded or captured. The ones who replaced them helped me but they were beat down and didn't take cover like we'd been taught to do and seemed not to care about anything. It was cold and rained every day. At night we were in muddy slit trenches or clammy, stinky cellars. Every attack resulted in a counter-attack. What misery, what awful misery!"

"It's amazing that we won the war," Tietje commented. "Not really, Lieutenant," Tex responded, "because in spite of this our soldiers kept on fighting. Also, the platoon leaders and company commanders were capable and brave. They led the way; that's why so many of them died. Besides, the Krauts were worse off and happy to surrender if their officers weren't close. In March, things got better."

"Not in my battalion," somebody countered. "Guys were cracking up from lack of sleep. Quite a few refused to do what they were told. That wouldn't have happened earlier. By then the fighting was almost over and we didn't want to get killed."

"Things were better for my company," Tex asserted. "We went into towns where everyone had fled and slept in their houses and cooked the food they left behind."

"Six of us were in a German home on Easter Sunday," a doughboy called Shorty declared. "The family was nice, so we didn't mess up the place. The mother and her 10-year-old son and 8-year-old daughter and her parents put on their best clothes and went to church. When they returned the grandmother prepared a meal and we all ate it together." Some families, he added, "were nasty or arrogant. We kicked them out and trashed their houses. It's too bad we had to keep destroying German cities and killing people, but the SS troops and Hitler Youth wouldn't surrender."

A private who looked like he couldn't be more than 18 told us he prayed regularly until a mortar shell "blew apart Slim," his buddy. "Slim was the most religious person in the squad and claimed the Lord would watch over him. I figured if this is how the Lord watches over us, something must be wrong, so I quit praying. And you know what? I didn't even get wounded. That's really strange, isn't it?" Nobody answered, and for a minute or two there was silence.

Murphy wanted to hear about our experiences as kriegies. When a captain referred to being in a medieval castle for 48 hours, I asked if it was at Diez.

"Yeah," he replied.

"Why didn't they keep you longer?"

"No reason to. I told them what little I knew and they released me."

Without thinking, I said, "Some guys refused to talk."

He shrugged his shoulders. "Maybe they knew important stuff, or maybe they talked but won't admit it."

I didn't say any more and Diez wasn't brought up again.

On our fourth day there the U.S.O. presented a variety show for troops in the Halle area. We attended and were laughing uproariously at a comedian when an officer interrupted him to announce that cargo planes had arrived and would fly a group of P.O.W.'s – "ex-P.O.W.'s, that is" – to Reims for "processing" prior to their departure for America. Those whose names he called must leave immediately. Mine was one of them. As we began filing out, everybody in the theater who had not been a kriegie rose and, facing us, applauded. Performers came from backstage to join in. It was a fabulous moment, one I've never forgotten. Here were people who understood what we'd been through, and cared.

Our treatment at Reims was equally good and we enjoyed the sightseeing opportunities it afforded. A letter to the family mentioned visiting

> *the cathedral, which is beautiful and impressive, the school house where the Krauts surrendered unconditionally, and a champagne factory where they let us sample their product. That glass of champagne was my first alcohol in a long while and it was enough; another and I'd probably have been doing handsprings down Rue de Foch. . . . I located several issues of "Time" and have read them. Also, believe it or not, I found a copy of the Omaha World-Herald. . .*

On May 27th we boarded a train for the overnight trip from Reims to Camp Lucky Strike. Bunks in hospital cars provided a place to sleep. Lucky Strike was a vast tent encampment where liberated P.O.W.'s and sick or wounded soldiers going home to recuperate were assembled for return to the States. The accommodations seemed fine to me: mattresses, sheets, pillows, showers with an unlimited supply of hot water, a well-stocked PX, barber shops, Signal Corps cable service, books, magazines, ping pong tables, movies, band concerts and U.S.O. programs. For ex-kriegies the food continued to be limited in quantity. A memo from the Chief Medical Officer said:

> *Most of you have been on a starvation diet. A diet consisting of coarse German bread and watery soup consumed over a period of weeks and months does something to your stomach and entire body. You have lost tremendous weight and there have been changes in your digestive system, skin and other organs. You are weak and susceptible to disease. All of you have had diarrhea and some still do. The reason is that you lack vitamins and the proteins*

so necessary in building healthy, solid tissues and muscles. The lining of your stomach is sore, delicate, inflamed and irritated. Your stomach has shrunk. If you load up that small, sore stomach, you may become acutely ill. . . .

It sounded like overkill to me but maybe he was just doing his job.

I sent the folks a Signal Corps message confirming my liberation: "A free man and sailing for home soon. Feel wonderful. Love. Bill." The following afternoon, unwilling to endure further uncertainty about whether Dad was alive, I sent a second one requesting that they cable me. I had to know.

We were given physical exams, interviewed regarding our capture and treatment, questioned concerning stool pigeons and informers, handed papers to fill out, and told we would leave for the United States "as fast as ships can make it here to take you." No answer came from my parents.

At the recreation center I bumped into Thiel, who had been a cubicle mate of mine at Oflag 64. That evening he described what happened after his departure from the march group at Eichfeld:

When the new guards showed up, another kriegie and I hid in a grove of trees for a couple of days, then started east, dodging both Germans and Russians. We did this for a week, until our food was gone, then went to a farmhouse and knocked on the door. The Polish family living there fed us and let us stay in a shed until we decided, several days later, to head for Warsaw. We walked part way and rode the rest in a Ruski army vehicle. The driver took us to a camp they had for P.O.W.'s and refugees. It was a dump, so we sneaked out and hitch-hiked and rode trains to Lublin, which somebody thought was the best city to go to. No one paid much attention to us when we got there.

After 8 or 9 days in Lublin, with meager rations and no decent place to sleep, a bunch of us were loaded into boxcars bound for Odessa. There was a stove in mine but no fuel for it, so I nearly froze until we managed to steal some wood during one of many stops. The Russians gave us food but it wasn't enough. I sold my blanket to a civilian and used the money to buy bread. Once we had a pretty good meal at a Ruski mess hall. That trip lasted a week.

In Odessa we were put in a structure that wasn't heated and didn't have running water. Food was supplied but they treated us poorly. Maybe the Krauts were right when they said America ought to be fighting the Russians.

Early in March an English vessel transferred us to Egypt, where we got showers, new clothes, medicine, money and a boat ride to Naples. Then my malaria flared up. I was in the hospital until last month and now am cleared to go home.

Lucky Strike was in the country, miles from anything of interest. Individuals or small groups, discouraged by assurances of departure that failed to materialize, often slipped away to Paris or some other city. I was arranging to do this – why not live it up a little! – when my name appeared on a list of those who would "leave for LeHavre tomorrow" and sail the next morning.

Our ship, the *Admiral Mayo*, designed to transport troops, had narrow, built-in iron-bar bunks that rose five-high. Reaching the top one, which I drew, required considerable agility and, once in it, ongoing alertness due to a large pipe that ran lengthwise just above my head. There were 5,000 of us aboard, in addition to the crew. A single breakfast, the mess officer stated, involved cracking 14,000 eggs by hand. I chatted with Sampson and others, lay in the sun, read, and one afternoon, looking down at the surging water, remembered the night I stood on a deck of the *Saturnia* hoping I would return. Now I was.

A variety of thoughts spun through my mind during that six-day voyage across the Atlantic. Had being overseas changed me? Not that I was aware of. In ways that weren't apparent? Perhaps. I recalled my decision to forgo visiting the gal Kaz told me about in Normandy. When a similar opportunity presented itself in Reims, I succumbed. Didn't that prove I'd changed? No; the circumstances were different; the war was over, the aggressor defeated. I recognized, however, that this might be rationalization. Both of them were young French women whose families needed food; why did the lieutenant who idealistically felt we came to help these people, not to take advantage of them, turn away the first time but acquiesce the second? Had his idealism been superseded, at least to some extent, by realism? Probably, but maybe this happens regardless of war.

How about my optimism – had war destroyed it? Would I now be grumpy, pessimistic, quarrelsome, morose? Are there mental scars – psychological wounds – I don't know about? This seemed unlikely.

Has America changed? Girls do work formerly done by men. Boys who grew up on farms and in small towns have seen the great cities of our country and the world. Will the way of life we fought to preserve disappear? Apparently I believed not; a note in my memo book says: "Eventually there will be peace and what I spent so long preparing for will begin."

I wondered if the folks' friends would look at me with disdain because I was captured. The troops by the Elbe cheered and shook our hands, those in the theater at Halle rose and applauded; but they were front-line soldiers. Will people at home consider us losers – failures – cowards? We didn't think of ourselves as failures, and certainly not as cowards, but realized that instead of leading our men to victory we had ended up prisoners. Though most of us believed it was either someone else's fault or a tough break for which nobody was to blame, we obviously had not been winners.

One day, in the ship's PX, a pfc. asked, "Are you Lt. Stevens?" He turned out to be an E Company soldier named Hernandez who, wounded in January, was on his way to a rehabilitation hospital. We talked awhile. Sabatini and Polk, he remarked, told Captain Kaznolwicz they thought I'd been ambushed.

It hadn't occurred to me that those enemy riflemen might have been lying in wait for a patrol to show up. Did that explain their sudden appearance? Was I ambushed? No, I decided after carefully reviewing all that took place; they were headed for the outpost. That I happened to be checking it just then was pure chance, a coincidence which seemed unfortunate at the time but may have saved my life.

Later I pondered whether it was wrong to feel that chance rather than a loving Heavenly Father kept me from being seriously injured or killed. Did those German soldiers with rifles pointed at my back not fire them because of God's intervention? Did He keep the shrapnel that nicked my leg from ripping apart my intestines, the bullet that went into Thompson's chest from tearing open mine instead? No, too many good men died. It was chance. God may have saved a few, but most of us who survived were lucky. Combat is a gamble, a roll of the dice. They rolled favorably for me.

I hoped they had rolled favorably for Kaz, Jud, Dorgan, Gray and Albertson. We worked hand in hand at Camp Campbell, on maneuvers, at Fort Jackson and overseas, cooperated, functioned as a team, shared successes and disappointments, good times and bad ones, and as a result were like brothers. Hernandez had heard that Kaz was alive but knew nothing about the rest.

I hoped the dice had also rolled favorably for Mahlin and the men of our platoon but knew that for a great many soldiers they didn't. Recalling the hundreds of dead Russians we saw during the march through Poland, and those in Luckenwalde's communal graves, I wondered why a beneficent Lord let so many perish. These people, too, were his children: did their lives have no value, were they of no consequence? The answer, I realized, was beyond my ability to comprehend. "The Almighty should not be blamed because we went to war instead of settling our problems peacefully," I noted in my memo book; but the number of deaths and vast amount of destruction troubled me.

The *Admiral Mayo* docked at Boston rather than New York. A military band played while we disembarked and Red Cross ladies distributed cloth bags containing toilet articles. Trains took us from there to Camp Myles Standish, where our stay was to be temporary – a week or less. Transportation to reception centers (in my case, Fort Leavenworth) had been requisitioned and orders granting 60-day leaves "for recuperation" signed. We were welcome to make use of the camp's PX's, clubs and theaters. Those who wanted to could call home; but the number of lines available was limited, so delay should be expected.

Dozens of officers and enlisted men were at the telephone exchange when I got there. "Your call cannot be completed for three or more hours because many are ahead of you," the operator stated. I left for awhile, then returned. Darkness fell. One by one, phones rang in the eight or ten booths located by the building. Somebody would answer, shout a name, and step aside when a soldier, materializing from the crowd, came forward. "Is Dad alive, is Mother, are they okay?" I asked myself as, for me, the moment of truth drew near.

It finally arrived. "Lt. Stevens?" the operator inquired.

"Yes," I replied, crossing my fingers.

"Go ahead, please."

"Bill!" two voices said in unison. Both of them were there; my concern had been unnecessary.

We couldn't cover much in the limited time each caller was allowed. They'd received my cables from Lucky Strike and quite a few of my letters. The cocktail shaker would be ready.

I supplemented our meals at Myles Standish with candy bars and chocolate malts, drank beer in the Officers Club, saw several movies, looked at old issues of *Time* magazine, and laughed out loud when I read that the week ending October 14, 1944, had been "uneventful" for the Third Army. For me it wasn't! When a fellow I'd known in ROTC reported that Chuck Mason and half a dozen others from our barracks at the library were killed in combat, I remembered Chuck's statement about not surviving.

The troop train that transported us to Fort Leavenworth spent hours on sidings. A streamliner carrying German soldiers in air-conditioned Pullman cars moved past us – P.O.W.'s our forces had captured, starting their journey back. It struck me as ironic that they were traveling in comfort while we rode in uncooled coaches without sleeping facilities.

Art and I got a lift from Leavenworth to a highway intersection near Nebraska City, where his parents and mine planned to meet us. A lot had happened in the ten months since my farewell to the folks at the railway station in New York. Will it seem like a miracle to them that I'm returning? It kind of did to me.

We embraced, stared at each other, talked a little, and visited briefly with the Sampsons. I didn't realize until later that both families were afraid to say much for fear of bringing up something which might trigger an adverse reaction in us and therefore shouldn't be mentioned.

"Want to drive?" Dad asked as we walked toward the car. "No," I answered, "but you should have seen me last September behind the wheel of an army truck in France." That opened the flood-gates; they wanted to hear everything. I related experience after experience, and was still at it when we reached Lincoln.

"How does it feel to get home?" Mother said as we approached our house. In what surely must rank as one of the greatest understatements in the history of mankind, I responded: "Pretty good!"

10

Their friends began stopping by that night, and the flow of visitors continued for many days. What interested them most was my incarceration in the castle at Diez. Again and again I told about the German NCO saying I might be shot as a spy, the officer who claimed to have worked in Columbus, the Red Cross food parcel he showed me, his assertion that America and its allies were winning the war and it would soon be over, the agonizing debates with myself about whether to answer his questions, the loneliness and uncertainty of solitary confinement. Everyone appeared to be entranced.

It quickly became clear that neither civilians nor servicemen considered capture a disgrace. For quite a few, the opposite seemed to be true: it was a mark of distinction. In their eyes P.O.W.'s suffered greater hardships than other soldiers and had persevered as a result of unparalleled courage. I relished the attention and reveled in the acclaim.

The folks explained how they learned that I was missing and, later, that I was a prisoner. On October 31st, Halloween evening, somebody rang their bell. Assuming it was children expecting treats, Dad picked up the candy jar. His heart sank when he opened the door and saw, standing there, Western Union's local manager. Ordinary telegrams were delivered by boys on bicycles, or telephoned, not brought by the man in charge. "I have a message for you, Mr. Stevens," he said. Mother joined him and they read it together:

The Secretary of War desires me to express his deep regret that your son Second Lieutenant William D Stevens has been reported missing in action since thirteen October in France. If further details are received you will be promptly notified. J A Ulio The Adjutant General.

They called Mike at West Point, informed relatives, and contacted the local newspapers. Letters of condolence poured in. "Don't give up hope" or "May God provide the strength you need to carry on" were frequent statements. Nearly all of them added, "We are praying for his safety." The mother of a missing pilot mentioned her many "hours of anguish — the seemingly endless days and nights — with always, always, stark reality in the back of your mind."

One of the letters was from Ginny. "I have fond memories of our many happy times together," the closing paragraph declared; "I loved him then and still do." I read it twice, remembering the joy we shared, and wistfully thought about what might have been.

In an effort to obtain more information, Dad wrote to the Adjutant General's office in Washington, to Colonel Scott, and to the YD chaplain. "We have heard that his division landed in France and was rushed into combat," he told Mike. "We are clinging to the hope that Bill is a prisoner."

"Clinging" was no doubt the right word to use. Mother confided to me that he believed I had died.

Colonel Scott answered his letter late in November:

We have an unconfirmed report that the Germans buried an American officer on or about October 14. The identity of this officer can be reduced to three, your son being one of them. . . .

You can be sure Bill performed a heroic act. He made three trips into enemy lines to gain important information essential to our movement forward. . . .

That wasn't encouraging but it gave him something to be proud of and tell his friends. He, Mother, Mike, who came home for Christmas, and David, who would soon be going into the navy, spent December 25th together not knowing whether I was alive.

"We drank a toast to you," David revealed later, "then all four of us cried."

On January 2nd Western Union delivered another telegram. It brought good news:

> *Report just received through the International Red Cross states that your son 2d Lt William D Stevens is a prisoner of war of the German government. Letter of information follows from the Provost Marshal General.*
>
> *Dunlop, Acting Adjutant General*

"What a difference a day makes," Dad wrote me that evening. "Everything is all right here and will continue to be now that we know you are safe."

"After such a long time with no word, it was difficult not to fear the worst," a letter from Mike confessed. "Were you wounded? The folks look years younger. It's been awfully tough on them."

"Not all parents who have endured the despair you did will be blessed with such a glad message," a relative commented:

> *I believe the horrors of war can never be erased from the minds of those whose boys are killed. . . .*
>
> *So many have not returned. I prayed that Bill would be saved and do hope, for your sake as well as his, that he won't be shipped to the Pacific.*

On January 8th they received one of my letters from Oflag 64; and in the weeks that followed, others arrived, though not in the order they were sent. "What a thrill to see your handwriting!" Mother's reply remarked; "We are the two happiest people in the world, knowing you are alive and well."

News of Oflag 64's evacuation decreased their happiness. "We are concerned because he is probably nearer to Berlin and the situation of the Germans is becoming desperate," Dad told his sister. A letter Mother wrote me in March said: "I wish there was some way of determining where and how you are. If we could just be assured that you are all right I would be so thankful. We try not to worry and to remain optimistic and have faith but it is hard to do." She and dad kept writing and sending packages, and each night asked God to watch over and protect me.

They had notified Kaz that I was a P.O.W. His answer reached them in April:

> *Received your most welcome letter. It certainly was a great pleasure to hear that Steve is all right. I need not tell you how well liked he was by everyone. I wanted to be like him, so happy and sure. I believed he was alive because I searched the area for his body . . .*

On May 8th, V-E Day, they attended a special church service. "Let us remember," the program said, "with pride, gratitude, love, sorrow and tenderness, the innumerable company of those whose courage and sacrifice made this hour possible. They died for us."

"What's become of our son?" Mother whispered plaintively. "He, too, helped make this hour possible. Why have we heard nothing from or about him? Has something terrible happened?"

"Months have passed since we were last told anything regarding these P.O.W.s," Dad declared in a May 15th letter to National Red Cross headquarters, "and the anxiety is almost more than some of the mothers can bear." He could have added, "or some of the fathers." A May 21st one to the Commanding General of Army Signal Corps, a man he knew slightly, asked, "Is there any way I can find out whether my son has survived?" Frustrated by lack of information, he sent the following to various officials:

> *On May 19th, SHAEF disclosed that negotiations were being carried on for the return of American prisoners liberated in Russian zones. It seems incredible that they have not yet been released and that further negotiations are required. Furthermore, apparently no information has been given to the next of kin of these prisoners.*
>
> *We believe our son was moved from Oflag 64 in Poland to Luckenwalde, just south of Berlin, but we have not heard from him for over four months nor been told anything by the War Department during that time. We understand the prisoners suffered greatly on their long march from Poland.*
>
> *Isn't it tragic that these soldiers who did so much for their country must remain in the custody of the Russians day after day while SHAEF negotiates for their release and our high-ranking army officers celebrate with their Russian counterparts the victory these young men helped win. . . .*

On May 28th my cable from Camp Lucky Strike was delivered to them, and a Red Cross notification of my liberation. "No one could have shown more courage than you two have through the dark days," a friend wrote mother when the newspaper reported that I'd been freed and would soon be home. A letter to her from Mike, who was taking flight training, said:

> *All that we've hoped and prayed for, for so many months, has come true at last. Our prayers have been answered and the Lord found time to look after Bill. I suppose we all had our doubts about his safety; I sure did. With all those stories about prisoners being killed and our lack of word from him, it was easy to imagine horrible things that could have happened. But I know none of us ever gave up hope. Right after you called me I took off and flew four consecutive loops and gave thanks.*

My 60-day leave was spent playing golf, swimming, talking with the folks and others, writing letters and reading. I considered preparing an account of kriegie life, but the requisite zeal, inspiration and desire weren't present.

The war against Japan concerned me. It appeared that invasion of their homeland would be necessary. The number of casualties expected was huge. Outlying islands would have to be seized; Japanese soldiers would remain on them, hidden in caves and camouflaged foxholes, to destroy our advancing riflemen. I didn't want to go there. What if they captured me? It would be impossible to endure, physically, mentally or psychologically, being a prisoner again. My supply of courage, which had been meager to begin with, was depleted. One war is enough.

Colonel Scott, responding to a note I mailed him, invited me to rejoin the division as a company commander when it returned to America. I appreciated his thoughtfulness but couldn't bring myself to accept. OCS was cranking out new shavetails; let them experience the missed meals, sleepless nights, endless marching, rain, mud, cold and discomfort of life in an infantry unit. What I wanted was a desk job at an established army post where we gathered for drinks at 5 each afternoon and lived in a modern BOQ.

The regimental Adjutant confirmed that a Silver Star had been awarded to me "for gallantry in action." I remembered Kaz saying, as we stood on the reverse slope of my hill the afternoon of October 13th, 1944, "Somebody from another battalion got a medal; maybe you will too." I knew I didn't deserve one and assumed that this was his way of expressing regret for asking me to go out there a third time, on a mission which though not considered dangerous – "Just a little reconnaissance patrol . . . Don't take any chances" – wasn't really important. With GI's constantly being killed or wounded, a missing rifle couldn't have mattered much, and what difference did it make whether the Krauts had or had not, at that point, reoccupied their outpost?

My records also listed, the Adjutant added, two other awards. A Purple Heart had been issued for wounds sustained in battle. That amazed me. For an insignificant calf injury? I didn't even go to the aid station; how did they know about it? The award which brought real satisfaction – made me truly happy – was my Combat Infantryman badge. That one I deserved.

I wished the Silver Star could be shared with those men of First Platoon who, by their bravery, earned it. Why did so many of them go above and beyond what duty required? Was it adrenalin? Patriotism? Pride? All three, perhaps, plus loyalty to their comrades, guys they hadn't known until Fate brought them together in Company E. Every soldier who leaves the protection of his foxhole to advance against hostile fire should receive a Silver Star, I felt. That takes courage. Those who do it are gallant.

Kaz got a Distinguished Service Cross for "brilliant, heroic leadership at Sarre-Union, France":

> *With complete disregard for his own safety, he repeatedly led fierce assaults against the enemy, exposing himself to fire to inspire and encourage his men. He personally killed many of the enemy in bold, daring action, and his fearlessness and skill were in great measure responsible for the capture of the town.*

"Bold, daring, fearless" – this was Kaz, all right; he'd been that way since I first met him at Camp Campbell.

Our battalion earned a Presidential Citation:

> *As the 26th Infantry Division moved ahead in its sustained advance across Lorraine to the Maginot Line east of the Sarre River, this Battalion of the 101st Infantry Regiment distinguished itself in combat against strong enemy resistance by an aggressive, determined and coordinated effort on the part of its members and by the superior and daring leadership of its officers and non-commissioned officers in the four-day period from 18 to 21 November 1944. . . . Although reduced to an effective strength of less than 300 men, the battalion continued its attack on the next objective. . . . In these combat operations, the intrepid infantrymen of this Battalion, through their extraordinary heroism, bold courage, and fighting determination, reflected the finest tradition of the Army of the United States.*

The significance of "reduced to an effective strength of less than 300" didn't escape me. That was a tremendous reduction. Would I, if not captured, have been among the ones who were able to attack the next objective? How many of them survived?

Mahlin wrote that the lieutenant who replaced me was killed ten days later. I wondered if he had come direct from OCS; it would be tough for an inexperienced officer to take over tested troops. Mahlin received a battlefield commission and served for two days as platoon leader before being seriously injured. He listed the names of First Platoon men who were killed, wounded or captured, and those hospitalized with trenchfoot or pneumonia. By late November, more than half of those in our original group (including all but two non-coms) were gone. "It wasn't the same outfit after that," he remarked. "The teamwork developed by our months of training disappeared. The replacements didn't know each other or us. Some of them were good soldiers, but many were not. Personnel sent from the Air Corps couldn't load an M-1 rifle."

Mulvaney was killed by a sniper. An artillery shell got the soldier who thanked me for dancing with his wife at the Fort Jackson party. Machine gunners mowed down Kinzer, who went with me on the night patrol to Xanrey. Sabatini lost part of a leg and for the rest of his life would walk on an artificial one. Schieffen lost an eye; Polk, part of his scalp. Mahlin would never again have full use of his left arm. Korinek, who was shot in the legs on our combat patrol, recovered and became a part of the kitchen crew. Cherney, who got drunk in Normandy, became platoon sergeant when Mahlin received his battlefield commission and did an outstanding job.

Kaz was the only one of Second Battalion's four company commanders who didn't die. Jud never returned. Dorgan recovered from his jaw wound, took command of G Company, and eventually was captured. Gray "got sick" and had to be evacuated. Albertson left with battle fatigue. Frank Beattie was killed. "He wanted so much to be a lawyer," his mother wrote in reply to a letter I sent her. Chuck Mason had planned to practice law, too. So had the second cousin who took me to dinner in Columbus during OCS; he lost his life in the Phillipines. Only for me would what each of us worked so hard for become a reality.

On August 6th an atomic bomb – something most people knew nothing about – destroyed a city in Japan. A few days later another city was destroyed and the Japanese agreed to surrender. I went to my room and, kneeling at the bedside, thanked God that World War II, which caused millions of deaths, untold destruction, and indescribable suffering, at last had ended.

Mother, Dad and I drove downtown. The streets were jammed with automobiles, their horns blaring, moving slowly or not at all. Pedestrians snaked between them and pranced along the sidewalks, hugging, kissing, shouting, singing, flashing with upraised fingers Churchill's "V for Victory" sign. After watching the festivities for half an hour, we inched our way out of the melee and departed.

Now and then, looking back, I remembered crouching in a foxhole while the earth around me trembled from exploding shells; the terror on that wounded German's face as I ran toward him; the night patrol to Xanrey in torrential rain; my hand sliding into Thompson's chest cavity; how scared I was crawling toward the Kraut outpost and my dismay when I saw those enemy soldiers behind me; my misery during the train ride to Oflag 64 and on the march through Poland; the cold, hunger and diarrhea that accompanied much of kriegie life. Most of the time, however, my thoughts were about the immediate future: where I would be sent next, whether my work would be hard or easy, pleasant or unpleasant; when military service would end for me and for every other person in the armed forces who wanted more than anything else to be a civilian again.

My orders were to report to the reclassification and reassignment center at Hot Springs, Arkansas, on August 27th. Mother let me take her car. "Officers," my first letter to her related,

> *are billeted in hotels leased by the army. I was having a beer in the Garden Room of mine when a Special Services officer introduced me to an attractive young lady named Barbara Lorton and asked if I would like to dance with her. I did, and we had dinner there with another lieutenant and his partner. I offered to drive the girls home — both of them live in Hot Springs with their parents — but the Special Services staff wouldn't let me.*
>
> *Today I was interviewed and my records brought up to date. Tomorrow I get a complete physical exam. My classifier believes I will be here ten days and on active duty someplace else until next spring or summer. I have to attend classes on Wednesday, Thursday and Friday but only in the morning. Afternoons and evenings are free.*
>
> *We can swim, boat and fish at a lake not far from us, and fry steaks furnished by Special Services for 30 cents. Close by is a golf course. I played this afternoon and shot a 96 – two 48's. Having a car is wonderful.*

That weekend there was a dinner dance in the Garden Room. I invited Barbara and picked her up. Sunday she and I played Bridge with a major and his wife, had supper with Sampson and Joe Keller, then went to an evening church service – "which goes to show you," a letter home proclaimed, "what an upstanding girl she is, to say nothing of my own sterling character."

Monday afternoon I golfed. Tuesday, following a tea dance, Barb and I had dinner with her mother, then saw a movie. We swam Wednesday afternoon. My orders came on Friday. I was assigned to the Infantry Replacement Training Corps (IRTC) at Camp Robinson, Arkansas, near Little Rock, and allowed two days – Saturday and Sunday – to get there.

Barbara and I ate in the Garden Room Saturday night. "It's been a lot of fun here," I wrote the folks before leaving Sunday morning:

This is by far the nicest treatment I've ever received from the army. Dating Barb has added to my enjoyment. She told me about a girl in Little Rock I can call. They were classmates at the University of Missouri.

Camp Robinson was expecting me. "You'll be a platoon leader in Company D," my regimental commander said, "but spend most of your time instructing. I'll give you a ride to their headquarters." On the way he stopped at an area where soldiers were drilling. The officer in charge, a captain, his face covered with sweat and dust, ran over, saluted and stated his name, as we had been taught to do in OCS. That impressed me. The Combat Infantryman badge on his fatigues did, too, and I decided to wear mine oftener.

The C.O. of Company D was pleasant but not energetic and outgoing like Kaz. His exec and the other platoon leaders were friendly. I was housed in a tarpaper hut with three lieutenants from a different company. One of them was a YD veteran who joined the division in December and contracted pneumonia when it was rushed north to help our forces in the Battle of the Bulge. "I have nightmares and wake up screaming," he warned.

A letter that evening described "the set-up":

Our C.O. takes the company wherever it goes during the day and looks after it. His exec does the paper work. The platoon leaders handle the instruction. Each of them is on a committee that trains the battalion's four companies in a particular subject. Consequently a platoon leader is rarely with his men and hardly knows them. There are 225 draftees in my company. Most of them are 18 years old and and have been in the army a couple of months. A few are having difficulty adjusting to this kind of life. 30 sergeants and corporals supervise them and help the training committees.

We start at 6 some days and at 7 on others, have an hour and a half off at noon, and finish at 5. There is some night work. Wednesday and Saturday afternoons (and Sunday, of course) are supposed to be free. I'll tag along with the C.O. the rest of this week, go to orientation school next week, and then serve on one or more training committees.

I telephoned Becky Martin and told her Barbara Lorton had

said to call. She reacted cautiously but invited me to have supper Sunday evening with her parents and her at their home. I did, enjoyed myself, and arranged a date for the following Saturday. "We went to a dance at Hilltop," my letter to the folks reported, "and had a good time."

> *Orientation school was easy except for the physical conditioning it included. That wore me out but may be the very thing I need. I'll be instructing for 8 hours on Monday, 12 on Tuesday and 4 on Wednesday. Thursday night I'm company duty officer and must be in the orderly room from 7 to 9 to help our trainees with any personal problems they have. Saturday I'm battalion duty officer.*
>
> *Thanks, Dad, for sending the article about law school reopening in January. I wish Uncle Sam would discharge me before then but it's not likely that he will because I don't have enough points. I picked up 5 more, however, for being in the battle of Central Europe. It lasted until May 8th. We were liberated before that and are therefore treated as having participated. Pretty neat, eh!*
>
> *Change is the byword around here. Many officers are getting out and many are heading for ports of embarkation. The regimental commander put me in for 1st Lieutenant but said not to count on it being approved quickly.*

The army allotted "points" for length of service, months spent overseas, combat awards such as the Silver Star and Purple Heart, battle stars earned, and having dependents. Those with enough points were eligible for discharge.

On Wednesday I was made C.O. of A Company. My exec outranked me but, being on limited service, wasn't eligible for a command position. The platoon leaders — Benning graduates — seemed well-trained and capable. Our non-coms were excellent. Each day I marched our trainees to where they listened to lectures, watched demonstrations, and practiced what they were learning about. Because of the rapid turnover in officers, I had to instruct now and then, and company matters kept me busy some evenings.

October 14th, the first anniversary of my capture, passed unnoticed by me but not by Dad, who "gave thanks that either the

Lord or Lady Luck brought you safely through that terrible war." I replied:

> *I too am thankful that I'm safely home and the war is over. I rarely think about those experiences and have no desire to remember them. Being a P.O.W. was tough – for me and for you. . . .*
>
> *Less than a year ago I was in solitary confinement with nothing but a paper-bound copy of St. Matthew, a pencil, and ointment for the wound on my leg. I memorized the Sermon on the Mount, drew house plans on the wall until my lead was used up, and re-lived every happy event of my entire life. I also dreamed, very realistically, that you had died. I forced myself to ignore the dream as a meaningless trick of the mind and found out how it feels to be hungry, cold, uncertain, lonely, discouraged, beat down and scared, all at the same time. . . .*

"It was a close race," a subsequent paragraph asserted, "but my bars turned to silver before my hair did. The promotion arrived yesterday. Our battalion commander delivered it to the orderly room. We grinned at each other like two Chessy cats as I opened the envelope. So I'm a First Lieutenant at last. Now for a discharge!"

Becky and I went out together almost every weekend and occasionally on Wednesdays. She was attractive, enthusiastic and fun. Her parents took us to their country club for dinner more than once and often had me come by for Sunday evening supper. Becky was in love with Jeff Ballantine, a navy pilot in the South Pacific, so our dates didn't involve any romance, although I sometimes wished they could. Eventually I got the impression that she felt this way also, which led me to consider whether I should try to muscle in on Ballantine and maybe marry her. That's what Ken did to me with Ginny and an ensign did to Hank with his fiancée. Why be Mr. Nice Guy? Jeff, I rationalized, was probably shacked up somewhere with an Oriental gal and didn't deserve Becky. I'd paid my dues; to hell with him.

Two things held me back. First, muscling in on somebody overseas seemed unfair – sort of disloyal to a guy who, like me, was still serving in the armed forces because he had to. Second, and no doubt far more important: much as I liked Becky and enjoyed being with her, I wasn't sure we would make a good pair. She was a Southerner; I, a product of the midwestern plains. Our feelings regarding certain basics were not the same. A bond like the one that drew Ginny and me together didn't exist.

"Company A has certainly improved," my Sunday letter home declared:

> *It's now the best in the battalion. I got three 2nd lieutenants yesterday, replacing the three who left last week for overseas. Two of the new ones are combat veterans; the third isn't, so I'll probably lose him soon. I may also lose my job soon. Our Adjutant, who is a friend of mine, told me that several captains are being assigned to the battalion. They will no doubt be given command of the companies.*
>
> *I received the American Theater of Operations ribbon (why, I don't know) and the Victory Medal, so I'm almost as decorated as an Air Corps officer. Unfortunately no points are allotted for either of these.*

My tour of duty at Camp Robinson, though devoid of any real pressure and definitely not difficult, wasn't satisfying or meaningful. "I've done a good job with this company," a November note to Dad said, "and have worked hard. Result: nothing – no praise, no consideration, no encouragement. I dislike the army system intensely and am waiting for the day I'm through. Gosh how I wish somebody would walk in and hand me a discharge."

The following afternoon they did. I had marched our platoons to a training area and was standing by the bleachers while they listened to an instructor. A corporal drove up in a jeep, jumped out and came over to me.

"Lt. Stevens?"

"Yes."

"Your discharge orders are at regimental headquarters, sir. You should go to the Separation Section as soon as possible."

I pulled off my helmet liner, threw it high in the air, and yelled "Hooray!" The instructor, stopping in mid-sentence, stared at me. So did everyone else.

"I'm being discharged," I sheepishly announced; and retrieving the helmet liner, hastened away.

Clearances and releases were required; getting out of the military is more complicated than getting in. The officer succeeding me as C.O. would have to receipt for property issued to the company. We had been short of various items when I took over, our supply sergeant reported, and still were; he could "cover this by borrowing." A couple of days later the transition was complete. In farewell remarks to our trainees, I urged them to be good soldiers and not forget the sacrifices made by others. After expressing appreciation to my officers and non-coms, I shook hands with each of them. We'd gotten along well but the camaraderie that existed in YD's Company E hadn't been present.

A major explained the advantages of remaining in the Reserve Corps. I listened politely, then replied without hesitation, "No thanks." When the last release was signed, I piled my belongings in the car and departed. Two and a half years earlier I had yearned for army duty to begin. Now I couldn't wait for it to end.

Will the life I'm returning to be the same as the one I left, I asked myself on the way home. Will my perspective be the same as it was before? An article Mother had shown me said, "Part of every boy is lost in war." It mentioned loss of trust, loss of reluctance to do harm, loss of faith that the worthy are preserved, loss of feeling that men are honorable. I wondered if this was true. Will I consider men less honorable – trust them less – because of the rating sheet affair at Benning? Because two guys stole my food when we were kriegies? That seemed unlikely. I remembered Dad talking to me in my teenage years about honesty. I hadn't revealed that four of us visited a house of prostitution to see what it looked like. When he found out from one of the other dads, he put his arm around my shoulders and said, "Was it nice? What color were the drapes?" – then added: "Don't go to places like that for the real reason, Bill; it's demeaning and the risk of disease is great. Marry a nice girl, then be a faithful husband and devoted father."

Should I tell him about the French gal in Reims? He'd get a kick out of it and think this was little enough reward for someone who'd been through what I had. Or would he? Maybe he'd feel that the boy he urged to be compassionate, generous and unselfish should have given her the cigarettes without accepting anything in return.

I'm the same person I was before, I concluded, despite a multitude of unforgettable experiences; and what lies ahead for me in Lincoln will not differ significantly from what growing up there led me to expect. My military service was a diversion, an interlude, a book to be closed now and never re-opened.

I drove until forced by weariness to stop, spent the night in a motel, arrived the next day, began wearing civilian clothes, signed up for law school, started working in Dad's office, and telephoned a girl I'd gone out with in college for a date. Why waste time!

Christmas was wonderful. No tears were shed, no gloom prevailed, as the folks, Mike, David and I toasted each other with Whiskey Sours, exchanged gifts, sang carols, and reminisced. "Too bad you didn't become a fighter pilot," Mike commented with a smile. "Sure is," I replied, and we both laughed. Later, sitting alone in front of the fireplace, staring at its dying embers, I wondered how the dice would have rolled if that had happened.

Attempts the following afternoon to prepare a narrative describing my experiences as a soldier and prisoner of war got nowhere. This will have to wait, I decided; what matters now is the future, not the past.

Mother gave me the letters I'd written the family and theirs to me that came back marked "Missing in action." I placed them in a cardboard box with my military records, insignia, medals and P.O.W. memorabilia, expecting to read not only this correspondence but also my kriegie diaries in a month or two. Thirty-five years went by before I did. By then both of my parents had passed away.

I planned to destroy the Nazi flag – it was something I wouldn't dare display – then decided to keep it, not as a souvenir of my imprisonment at Luckenwalde but as a personal memorial to the Jews and thousands of other innocent people who were exterminated by Hitler – as a tangible "lest we forget" reminder of man's inhumanity to man.

Two of my old friends and I spent New Years Eve together at the Legion Club. We drank champagne, devoured *hors d'ouvres*, sang, and at midnight soberly raised our glasses when the master of ceremonies proposed a silent toast to those "still serving our country and those who never again will be able to serve it." At two a.m., walking from the garage to the house, I recalled the many times I crept along darkened hillsides in France. Maybe I have changed, I said to myself; I'm no longer "leery" of the dark. Whether someone is hiding nearby or sneaking forward no longer concerns me, and never again will.

Because of accumulated leave, my discharge was effective January 1, 1946. A few days after that, the Commanding General of Army Ground Forces thanked me for contributing to "the defeat of our enemies":

> *As you return to civilian life, you take with you the deepest appreciation of a grateful Nation and a grateful Army.*
>
> *In the years to come, I am sure you will look back with justifiable pride in the service you rendered your country.*

It was a form letter – no doubt everybody who served received one – but it was addressed to me and the fact that lots of others were getting a similar message didn't make any difference. I put it with my war mementos and on a slip of paper wrote what were to be, for a long, long time, my final words regarding World War II:

> *I was not a hero, but accepted the hard life of an infantryman, faced enemy soldiers in combat, endured the privations of a P.O.W., and throughout my military career – as an ROTC cadet, as an officer candidate at Fort Benning, as a platoon leader in the Yankee Division, and as C.O. of a replacement training company at Camp Robinson – conscientiously tried to do my best. Does that entitle me to look back on my service with justifiable pride? It probably should. I guess it does. I hope that's right. I'm sure glad it's over with.*

Epilogue

I became an attorney, married Kim Bates, had three children, participated in community affairs, and for many years kept a supply of candy bars in my desk drawer. Dad, remembering the vow set forth in one of his letters — "If God brings you safely through, the rest of my life will be filled with efforts to show my gratitude" — played an active role in the church, helped me in every possible way, and with no expectation of recompense or reward gave generously of his time and talents to those in need. My brother Mike was killed when his fighter plane crashed on a training mission during the Korean conflict. Dad died of heart failure in 1959.

In the late summer of 1962, Kim and I visited the area northeast of Nancy where YD went into combat. We found the tree-lined lane my platoon moved along in the darkness, the finger of land from which our first attack began, and the village we entered unopposed; drove our rented Volkswagen down the main street of Xanrey; and eventually located the small hill the platoon was on when Kaz told me to force the enemy from their outpost and "capture one if you can." Nothing indicated that in 1944, soldiers occupied foxholes here.

From its summit I studied the terrain to the east, then walked to where the outpost was and saw no evidence that it ever existed. A farmer plowing a nearby field peered in my direction. I waved, but he either didn't notice me or chose to ignore the greeting.

From there I strolled over to where our combat patrol must have been when those two unsuspecting Germans approached us, wandered around, recalled clearly all that happened that night, and in memory of Thompson quietly said what I failed to tell him then: "I'm sorry, Tommy. God bless you."

Kim was waiting for me in a grassy spot on the hill. She had brought bread, cheese and wine for a picnic. Clouds dotted the sapphire sky, a breeze blew gently, a bird chirped, cattle grazed contentedly in an adjacent pasture. It had not been this peaceful 18 years ago, nor the weather this lovely. Gazing at the knoll, the ridge behind it, the woods in no-man's-land that Sabatini, Polk and I returned through after our second trip, and the rolling countryside surrounding us, I thought about the men of First Platoon. What's become of those who survived? Do any of them remember this hill? Do they remember me? Do they remember the death and destruction they witnessed? It's a good thing we were young and tough, resilient and willing to risk our lives, I mused; otherwise we wouldn't have been able to do what we did.

It occurred to me, as I sat there reminiscing, that the only time I experienced overwhelming fear was while crawling on my stomach to that now-gone outpost. Fear had been present the previous week when we ran forward in our initial attack, but I had too much on my mind to be more than vaguely conscious of it. I was scared when one of my captors put the muzzle of his rifle against my spine and I believed he was going to kill me, but that lasted only a moment. When I lay at the crossroads on our march through Poland and assumed I was dying, my emotion was sadness rather than fear — sadness that the body which had served me so faithfully was giving out and life must end in this manner. Edging all alone through the darkness toward a hole in the ground some intelligence officer considered important, convinced that bullets were about to tear me apart, I was truly afraid. Smiling, I reached for the wine bottle. My fear had been unnecessary. The outpost hadn't been reoccupied. No one was there.

We went next to Diez. The front portion of the castle, now a museum, was closed, its entrance padlocked. The back part appeared to be some kind of detention center or group home. "No Admittance," a sign (in German) stated, but the door was ajar.

"Shall we go in?" Kim asked.

I hesitated, then decided it was foolish not to. Stairs led to an upper floor. We stole up them and came to a hallway. A male voice, loud, brusque and authoritative, could be heard in a nearby room. Ascending more steps, we found ourselves by the corridor I traversed many times. Memories of those days engulfed me as I walked uneasily, almost fearfully, to what once was my cell. The metal door had been removed, the stone walls plastered and painted, the furniture replaced; otherwise it looked the same. I slipped over to the window and glanced down at the town square. A sign on one of the buildings said, "Erich Kunkel," just as it did before.

My uneasiness increased. Would we be arrested for trespassing? Detained? Thrown in jail? Suddenly the *deja vu* became too much for me. "Let's get out of here," I whispered to Kim. Though surprised, she didn't argue. When we reached the lower staircase a man wearing black army boots, dark pants and a white T-shirt emerged from an office. I pretended to be examining pictures on the wall. He growled, "Verboten," plus a bunch of words I didn't understand. I understood the Verboten, however, and taking Kim by the arm hurried away.

We roamed around Diez, had a beer in one of its taverns, stayed all night at a *Gasthaus* by the Rhine, visited Reims, and drove from there to the beaches where Allied troops landed on D-Day. I climbed into German pillboxes and similar fortifications on the high ground above them, marveled at the bravery of those who attacked these positions, then went to the nearby cemetery. Tears ran down my cheeks as I stared at the rows of crosses and Stars of David that mark the final resting place of American servicemen whose hopes, dreams and lives came to an end on this foreign continent. "They're all equal here," I commented to Kim, observing the levelness of the ground and evenness of the grass; "nobody is higher or lower than the one next to him. That's the way it ought to be." I searched for Thompson's grave but was unable to find it, and learned later that he and 480 other YD soldiers are buried at St. Avold, east of Metz.

Carved into the wall of a pavilion at the Normandy cemetery was a map on which arrows showed the forward sweep of our advancing armies. I looked at the arrow by Nancy a long time, aware that an infinitesimal speck of it represented my platoon – and me.

Did the satisfaction that came from serving overseas exceed the misery involved, I asked myself. Yes, since everything turned out all right; but it wasn't worth the gamble – the risk was too great. I could have ended up beneath one of those crosses, my dream of practicing law, having a wife and children and being active in the community unrealized. Also, it caused my parents needless suffering. I should have done what Mother urged and Dad clearly wanted: opted for a rear-echelon spot or, with help from an influential friend of theirs, sought a safe assignment in the States. In my heart, though, as I stood with my eyes on the arrow near Nancy, I knew why I ignored their wishes. Tennessee maneuvers made me a part of E Company. To leave it, to not share what we trained together for so diligently, would have been both disloyal and dishonorable, qualities Dad taught me to abhor. "I had to do it, folks," I said, turning slowly from the map; "there wasn't any other choice."

In 1983, I read the letters they sent me that were returned undelivered, and mine to them; then, using a magnifying glass to decipher the faded writing and incomplete sentences of my Oflag 64 and Luckenwalde diaries, typed on sheets of paper what was recorded in them. I also began reading books written by former kriegies, and was amazed to discover that our captors were supposed to feed us the equivalent of what their own troops got, that third-degree tactics and physical abuse were prohibited, that P.O.W.'s had rights, that a Code of Conduct existed which encouraged "passive resistance" by prisoners of war. Why hadn't this been passed on to me? Then I remembered: the Geneva Convention and what you should do if captured were discussed during the final week of OCS, the week my squad missed, and at Fort Jackson the Friday I went to West Point.

Would threatening the guy from Columbus with retribution later on if he didn't give me a Red Cross parcel and arrange my release from solitary confinement have accomplished anything? Probably not, but one can't be sure. Recalling the captain at Halle who told "what little" he knew, I wondered whether it was foolish of me to delay disclosing which infantry regiments were in YD. My interrogator must have already possessed that information; according to *The Lorraine Campaign*, published by the army's Historical Division, secret agents in France regularly reported to German intelligence officers the location and strength of U.S. units. Also, by their "extremely careless use of telephones and radios," so did our own people.

Were some interrogators more lenient than mine? Is that why many kriegies remained in solitary confinement only a day or two? Or was it because they talked? Several admitted answering the questions asked of them. "What difference did it make?" one stated. Most never said whether they answered or not.

Eisenhower's Lieutenants, by Russell Weigley, broadened my perception of what took place in the European Theater of Operations. War, for generals, wasn't the same as it was for us. They had beds, ate gourmet meals, measured success by miles advanced and objectives seized regardless of how many lives were lost, and devoted considerable energy to justifying or covering up their mistakes. Very few of them saw the wounded writhing in agony, heard the anguished cries of those who were dying, or walked by lifeless bodies. Why, in the Hurtgen Forest and elsewhere, were infantry companies whose men trained side by side and knew each other given unrealistic missions that destroyed them? Why were so many GI's needlessly sacrificed, their expertise wasted? Patton's Third Army, in thc month of October, had more than 14,000 casualties – one of whom was me. YD's casualties from September through May totaled 18,950, well over 100%.

Another book revealed that high-ranking officers often showed greater concern for their own comfort than for the welfare of front-line soldiers. Rank has its privileges, but taking advantage of those privileges when your troops are suffering doesn't improve morale and reflects poorly on the commanders who permit it. They demanded a lot from us; we had a right to expect a lot from them.

I was lucky to be an officer. My privates and non-coms led a harder life than I did. America emerged victorious because these men – and others like them in all branches of the armed forces – bravely and loyally did what they were asked to do.

Once in awhile, lying in my comfortable bed, clean, warm and well-fed, I recall the countless nights I slept on muddy ground or didn't sleep at all, how cold I was at times, and my unending hunger as a kriegie. But those days are long gone and don't readily come to mind – except when the band plays our national anthem before a football game. Then, standing bare-headed with my hand over my heart, watching the Stars and Stripes wave in the breeze, I think about World War II and those who participated in it. Each of us, while performing the role assigned him, gave up the right to pursue other goals, to go where he wanted to go, to seek fulfillment in his own way. That's why our wartime service was so meaningful: we were doing something for others, something above and beyond ourselves, something from which we had nothing to gain and much to lose. That's why taking pride in it is justifiable. This is our recompense for the sacrifices we made, for the hardships we endured. Those were not our happiest years, nor our most rewarding, but they are years none of us will ever forget. And as we alone know, in some ways they were our greatest years.

HEADQUARTERS
ARMY GROUND FORCES
OFFICE OF THE COMMANDING GENERAL
WASHINGTON 25, D. C.

10 January 1946

First Lieutenant William D. Stevens
7955 East Benson Street
Lincoln 38, Nebraska

Dear Lieutenant Stevens:

During the world conflict in which our Nation has been involved, the Army Ground Forces performed its mission with speed and thoroughness. That success was an important factor in the defeat of our enemies and in the preservation of our beloved country.

I want you to know that I appreciate your personal contribution.

As you return to civilian life, you take with you the deepest appreciation of a grateful Nation and a grateful Army.

In the years to come, I am sure you will look back with justifiable pride in the service you rendered your country.

Sincerely,

Jacob L. Devers

JACOB L. DEVERS
General, USA
Commanding

August, 1943 - OCS *November, 1944* - P.O.W.
June, 1945 - Lincoln (with David and Mike)

November, 1945 ➤

PHOTOS COURTESY OF THE AUTHOR

U.S.
U.S.
101
101

Glossary

Appel	A formation required by German commanders to determine whether all P.O.W.'s under their control were present or accounted for.
ASTP	Army Student Training Program
BAR	Browning Automatic Rifle
beaucoups	French for "many" or "lots of"
C.O.	Commanding Officer
CP	Command Post. A front-line lieutenant's foxhole was usually his CP.
Exec	Executive Officer. The Exec was second-in-command in infantry companies, battalions and regiments.
FA	Field Artillery
Feldwebel	German sergeant
G I	Government Issue. Enlisted men were frequently referred to as GI's.
G-2	The Intelligence Officer of a division
IRTC	Infantry Replacement Training Corps
kaputt	German for broken or spoiled. Used by me ("Our food is kaput") to mean "all gone."
KP or k.p.	Kitchen Police: enlisted men assisting the kitchen crew
Kriegie	Kriegsgefangener (German for prisoner of war)
M-1	Model 1. An infantryman referred to his M-l (Garand) rifle as his M-1.
NCO	Non-commissioned officer (usually a sergeant or corporal)
OC	Officer Candidate
OCS	Officer Candidate School
Oflag	German prisoner of war camp for officers
P.O.W.	Prisoner of war
PX	Post Exchange
ROTC	Reserve Officers Training Corps
S-2	The Intelligence Officer of a battalion or regiment
S-3	The Operations Officer of a battalion or regiment
S-4	The Supply Officer of a battalion or regiment
SHAEF	Supreme Headquarters, Allied European Forces
Shavetail	2nd lieutenant
Six-by-six	U. S. Army truck with six wheels, all powered
Stalag	German prisoner of war camp
verboten	German for "prohibited" or "forbidden"